MW00977449

Great Practices, Great Games

Coaching Youth Baseball

**Foreword by
Frank Thomas**
of the Chicago White Sox

by Dr. John Mayer and
Steve Hayward

II

©1999 Coaches Choice Books. All rights reserved. Printed in the United States.

No part of this book may be reproduced, stored in a retrieval system, or transmitted in any form or by any means, electronic, mechanical, photocopying, recording, or otherwise, without the prior permission of Sagamore Publishing, Inc.

ISBN: 1-57167-392-x

Library of Congress Catalog Card Number: 99-64108

Cover Design: Jennie Scott

Interior Design: Janet Wahlfeldt

Editor: David Hamburg

Production Manager: Michelle A. Summers

Coaches Choice Books is a division of: Sagamore Publishing, Inc.

P.O. Box 647

Champaign, IL 61824-0647

Web Site: http//www.sagamorepub.com

Dedication

To my family. To Deborah, my wife, who always goes to bat for me. To Courtney, our first ball player and a young lady hitting home runs in life. To Justin, who we have watched develop into a good ball player and a great young man. To my dad, who was the first coach I had. To my mom, who always let me play. And to all the young people I have coached in many ways throughout the years and all those great coaches I had traveling through life.

Dr. John Mayer

Chicago, Illinois

I would like to dedicate this book to my dad, Cy, who, after working two jobs and being a father to five children, always had time to play catch with me and teach me the game; to my mom, who also taught me never to give up; to my pony coach, Jim Corso, who taught me how to treat players and made me want to coach someday—I also stole his sense of humor, and that has made me a better teacher of kids; to Larry Gray, who has helped me along the way; and to my colleague Scott Nelson, the founder and owner of Strikes Baseball Academy, who is the main reason why I am living my dream.

Steve Hayward

Oak Park, Illinois

Acknowledgments

The one constant through all the years, Ray, has been baseball. America has rolled by like an army of steamrollers; it has been erased like a blackboard, rebuilt and erased again. But, baseball has marked the time. This field, this game, it's part of our past, Ray. It reminds us of all that was once good and could be again. Oh, people will come, Ray, people will most definitely come.

—James Earl Jones to Kevin Costner,

from the movie *Field of Dreams*

We would like to thank Strikes Baseball Academy of Broadview, Illinois; the De La Salle Institute Baseball Program, Chicago; John O'Connor, director of the North Pier Athletic Club, Chicago; Scott Nelson, owner and head pitching coach of Strikes Baseball Academy; the Stan-Mil Mitt Company; the Hayward and Mayer families for their patience while we worked to complete this project ahead of schedule; and Tony Frankos for his support.

We would also like to give a special thank-you to our models: Justin, Emily, Vince, Jeff, and Adam.

Justin, Jeff, Vince , Emily and John Mayer (Adam is not in picture)

Contents

Introduction

The object of this book is to help adults with the important and sometimes ominous task of coaching a youth baseball team. These teams usually range in level from T-ball through high school; however, we believe that even college coaches can benefit from our approach to young people, even though our baseball mechanics may be a bit elementary for them.

The motivation to write this book arose out of the great need for a handbook to assist the armies of adults who find themselves in the position of coaching baseball each spring.

The baseball backgrounds of these adults are just as varied as their socio-economic backgrounds. As a result, many adults find themselves in the position of coaching young people, even though they have had no previous experience with the task.

These adults play a role in the lives of our children that may change some of these young people forever. Such an important role calls for the best support available, and, until now, that support has focused primarily on game strategy and tactics.

Often, their lack of coaching experience requires these adults to use what little time they have to work on game preparation—not on team practice or organization. Although handbooks, instructional tapes, and videos are available to help coaches with game strategy, until now, no resource has been available to help them run effective practices and handle the other collateral roles and duties that come with coaching. These roles and duties include, among other things, coping with parents and fans, disciplining players, working with sponsors, motivating players, and developing team cohesion. For these reasons, youth-league coaches should find this book to be an invaluable tool that will make their job much easier.

Although readers may have a tendency to go right to our illustrations, we recommend that they read and study the text carefully. The richness of our techniques is amplified by the detail given in the words on the pages that follow. Coaches should use this book as a reference. As such, we suggest that all the adults involved with a youth-league team obtain a copy.

Finally, as adults embark on this journey of teaching youngsters about the great game of baseball, they should enjoy the privilege of touching the lives of young people. We wish all the coaches good luck with a memorable season.

—John Mayer and Steve Hayward, 1999

Foreword

Most fans see me at the plate, attacking pitches and doing my job as a professional ballplayer. What they haven't seen are the many obstacles that I have faced just to get the opportunity to stand up at the plate.

In sports, I have always loved baseball first; but, like many of the loves in one's life, great disappointment has accompanied great success. I was not drafted by a major league team, nor was I offered the college scholarship for baseball that I so dearly wanted, coming out of high school. With exceptional college seasons in baseball and a very good performance in the 1987 Pan American Games, I still wasn't asked to be on the U.S. Olympic team. And although, as a minor leaguer, I had outstanding A and AA seasons and a great rookie spring training with the White Sox, I still wasn't brought up to the big leagues at the start of the season. My whole career seemed like a case of working to climb the mountain harder than anybody else, and yet never becoming king of the hill.

Throughout all of these obstacles, I kept working hard and not giving up. This work ethic came directly from my parents, as my dad worked two jobs all of his life, but it was reinforced by the coaches who influenced me as a youngster.

I was blessed to have coaches who were both teachers of baseball and mentors in life. I spent my childhood years shuttling between the local Boys' Club and my Little League. I was coached by men who spent a great deal of time not only with me, but also with all of the kids on their teams. They not only instilled in me a great work ethic toward sports, but they also made the work fun.

I'll never forget how my Little League coach got me to play center field, a position that most kids didn't want to play. He gave a speech to the team, which I later found out was directed mainly for my ears. In his speech, he declared center field our "glory position" and told me personally after the speech that, as the center fielder, I could roam all over the field and be the "playmaker of the team." After this "glory position" description, you couldn't hold me back from playing center field. I worked so hard at that position that I was throwing hitters out at first base on balls hit to me on a hop.

My coaches always taught me to continue to believe in myself, despite disappointment. They showed me lessons that I have been able to use throughout my career and my life. I learned focus, intensity, and teamwork from my coaches.

This book is for those coaches who guide young people at all levels, from T-ball through high school. This book embodies the direction and principles that I learned along the way to fulfilling my dream of playing in the major leagues. I hope that this book can prepare coaches and parents to better understand how to guide young people. Sure, it's a book about baseball, but it is also a book about being a good adult role model while using baseball as your tool.

Enjoy and learn from this reading.

Frank Thomas

Chicago White Sox

Chicago, Illinois

1999

The Prototypical Coach

Great head of hair (for frequent pulling out)

Eyes of a hawk

**Voice of an opera singer
(for yelling above the crowd)**

Heart of a lion and a saint

Hands of Hank Aaron

**Stomach of cast iron
(not only for tolerating
tension, but for eating
kid's food all season)**

**Mind of a
psychologist
teacher
parent
policeman
poker player
strategist**

**Arms of Arnold
Schwarzenegger
(for carrying the team)**

Good Shoes

Clean socks

Chapter 1

Adult Attitudes

SETTING THE TONE FOR YOUR TEAM

Anyone who has been around groups of young people can tell you that they are the best psychologists in the world. They watch us adults like hawks. Our mannerisms, our dress, our speech, the way we behave are all soaked up by youngsters as they try to figure out our world. In fact, figuring out our world seems to be the primary task of youngsters everywhere. No wonder they are so good at it.

This goal of young people to figure out our world also means that all adults play an important role in guiding the lives of youngsters, whether we realize it or not. When adults assume the role of leadership in their relationships with young people, they set the tone for their group. In coaching, this adult leadership is magnified, because it is in the arena of sports that children most often look to adult leadership for help.

Typically, youngsters join a baseball team so that they can play and have fun. When you think about it, that same eagerness doesn't readily exist in the school, the home, the church, or the other settings in which adults try to influence young people. Considering this combination of young people's constant scrutiny and their eagerness to follow the examples set by coaches, it is critical that coaches think about the tone they are setting for their teams. It is important that coaches understand that the tone they set will be locked in on by their players. If coaches use a negative tone, they'll have a negative team. If they act like tough guys, they will create a team of tough guys. Conversely, if they emphasize enthusiasm, energy, and fun, then their team will be eager to play and have a good time doing it.

The ideal tone to set with your team is one that is positive, that emphasizes fun, that stresses the importance of respecting fellow players, coaches, umpires, and the other teams as well. Coaches should be advocates for their players—not cheerleaders. When players strike out, their coaches should let them know they will have another chance. Coaches should refrain from getting down on their players. Instead, they should their players what they did wrong—but in a positive, mentoring way. Such an approach is realistic—not Pollyannaish. It shows respect for the players, a respect that will be returned in kind. Coaches who rip into their players and tear them down will provoke a negative, counterproductive reaction from these youngsters.

Remember that playing baseball yields a high degree of failure.

More than any other sport, baseball accepts failure as simply a part of the game. We are all familiar with the statistics. A good batting average is around .300, which means that good hitters fail on two-thirds of their tries. A great pitcher has an earned run average below 2.50. At the major league level, good teams measure success by how many games they have won above the .500 level. These global measures of failure are an accepted part of baseball lore. Unfortunately, they do not necessarily get translated down to the youth level. Many youth coaches expect perfection, yet baseball is not a game of perfection.

A coach must learn how to accept failure and use it as a learning tool.

GAINING THE RESPECT OF YOUR PLAYERS

Mutual respect between coaches and players provides the perfect chemistry for coaches to work with the modern ball player. Many coaches do not understand this fact. These coaches are operating as if they are handling the same players they played with so many years ago—but those players are long gone. You can say many things about today's youth, but one fact that endures is that youngsters thrive on respect.

The key ingredient in getting respect from youngsters is to give it.

Other essential ingredients in establishing respect on your team include the following: establishing discipline, setting limits, establishing boundaries between coaches and players, listening to your players, communicating with your team, not tolerating horseplay, setting rules, and being a role model.

TEAM DISCIPLINE

Establishing discipline is such an essential aspect of team building that it requires special attention. The most important point for coaches to keep in mind is that they should set team rules, follow them, and be consistent in following them. They should never make exceptions to their rules; inconsistency is pure poison when handling young people. Many coaches sacrifice consistency in their rules for winning, and that type of trade-off *always* comes back to haunt the coach. The biggest mistake coaches make when they try to discipline their players is to allow the gifted players to be exceptions to the rules. A seasoned coach knows that gifted players come and go. Achieving good team chemistry is more important, more powerful than pleasing a talented player.

Coaches should make sure they communicate their rules clearly. To help promote good communication to their players, coaches should write down a list of rules and then go over them with the players. They should then send a copy of the rules to the parents of the players and also do what teachers do—have the parents sign the list and send it back to the coach. This procedure helps coaches know that their rules are being taken seriously. Writing the rules down not only helps establish team discipline, but it also makes coaches more responsible and fair.

How exactly can a coach enforce team rules? Coaches must realize that they have a great deal of clout over their players. The most obvious way to enforce a rule is to bench the player who breaks it. What may be a secret to coaches is that children still listen to adults. If you are firm and treat your players with respect and fairness, then they will listen. Young people do not listen to adults who are not fair, or who play favorites. Coaches should never look the other way when it comes to enforcing rules.

Because young people will test a coach early and often to see if he or she actually intends to enforce the rules, it may appear to the coach that he or she needs to be stricter early in the season. Coaches should not be discouraged if their players test them. Most important, they should never let their guard down.

Another method of enforcing team rules is a system of fines. Let's be realistic here, however: We are discussing youth baseball from T-ball through high school, so these players can't be expected to have money. Money is only one way to establish a system of fines. How about making field cleanup a consequence for a rule violation? Coaches can assign their players a number of minutes of cleanup for breaking a rule. Let's face it, even if coaches fine their players a small sum of money, most probably that money will come from their parents. As a result, the consequence of the rule violation will be diminished. Practically every youngsters hates to have to do chores. Therefore, coaches who punish their players by making them pull weeds, pick up trash, or rake the field may soon see their players towing the line. A nice plus to the use of consequences such as cleanup will be that the baseball field will be cleaner. Furthermore, a clean field makes players proud and motivated to play. Hence, this system of punishment offers a great deal of benefit all the way around.

Of course, a traditional method of enforcing rules is to have players perform a physical consequence, such as running a lap around the park. As much as they hate chores, players loathe running laps, sprinting, doing push-ups, etc. However, we have some words of caution for coaches who like to use such methods as consequences for breaking rules:

First, don't just employ these methods because that is what you had to do as a player. Your discipline system has to fit your team. For example, very young players, ages six to eight, may not be physically developed enough to make a physical consequence meaningful. Have you ever seen a six-year old try to do a push-up? This problem holds true for running as well. Oftentimes, running becomes a time for showing off or attention getting—unless you monitor it closely—and then that diverts your attention from the rest of the team. Physical consequences will become playtime for the younger players. For players six through eight, cleanup is more effective. Another important point is to have these younger players do the conse-quence immediately. Why? Because we adults forget that children's concept of time is very different from ours. The experience of time is longer for younger children and becomes shorter and shorter the older a person gets. For this reason, children this age respond best to immediate feedback rather than a delayed response. To a child between the ages of six and eight, doing something sometime later for bad behavior causes his punishment to become disconnected from his bad behavior. If a player this age breaks a rule, you should stop his (not the whole team's) practice and make him clean up a part of the playing field away from the practice. Usually, the rule violation at this age will involve some kind of stimulus that the child is responding to; hence, your consequence of cleanup will also remove the child from the interference of that stimulus.

Second, using physical consequences runs the risk of injury. A tired body is the most vulnerable to injury. Making a player run and then resume practic-ing may increase the chance of injury. Older players are less of a problem in this regard, as their bodies are more mature and better developed. There-fore, it makes much more sense to employ a physical consequence on older players. Also, older players may relish field cleanup instead of running or push-ups.

Third—and it is unfortunate that we have to think like this today—employ-ing physical consequence at the wrong age increases your chances of having conflicts with parents. Although you are within your rights to establish your own rules and discipline system, by using physical consequences for younger players, you also run the risk of inviting a confrontation with a parent. Why risk the bother? Getting into arguments with parents wastes your time when you could be employing other effective consequences.

Fourth, on the positive side of physical consequences, the older player who is being punished with physical exercise will improve his conditioning. As the coach, however, you must be fair and steer clear of pushing the older player too far—again, because of the chance of a fatigue injury. The fact that you have rules—and will enforce those rules often—can serve as ample warning to your players that they should behave themselves.

During one high school game, the coach made the players who were on the bench run a lap because they were not paying attention to the game. Well, a grandmother could have run faster than those players ran that lap, but his consequence worked. For the remainder of the game, those players paid attention. So you see, adults often forget how much power they have in young people's lives. Often, it is not the severity of the consequence you are administering, but just the fact that you are administering it, that obtains the desired result in your players.

Fifth, physical consequences can probably be used immediately, without disrupting the other players' practice. Even though older players' concept of time is more adult-like than that of the T-ball player, the older player still is more driven by the need for instant gratification than an adult. If a player violates a rule, employ your consequence immediately. Have them run right now—not after practice. Doing a consequence within the time frame that the offense occurred magnifies the effect of the consequence. Conversely, a consequence is diluted when it is done a long time after the offense is committed.

To review methods of discipline, let's chart what works. On the next page is a sample list of team rules. Following this list of rules is a chart that shows age-appropriate guidelines for implementing consequences for rules violations. This system of rules and consequences works. It was used to take a team of 11-year-olds with a record of 12-20 and turn them into a championship team of 12-year-olds with a record of 31-2. Of those two losses, one was a forfeit that resulted from several team members playing meteorologist (see rule No. 10, which will be discussed later in this book). By the way, the "Tigers" is a hypothetical team name used for our examples.

Team Rules

- We are **Tigers** so we can have fun, play hard, be a part of a team, and become better baseball players.

- Playing well takes practice. Our practices are important, and you cannot miss practice unless excused by Coach Hayward or Coach Mayer.

- We joined the **Tigers** to play games. If you have to miss a game, you must inform us well ahead of time so we can prepare for your absence.

- Arrive on time for all practices and games. Great players have a habit of arriving 15 minutes before the time the coaches announced.

- You will be told what to wear for practice. You will be given a uniform for games. You must wear the practice uniform for practice or the complete game uniform for games. You do not play or practice unless you are dressed appropriately.

- For boys, a cup supporter must be worn at all times for practice and for games. Girls must have their chest protector on at all times.

- The league rules allow 2 weeks of vacation time from the team. (Note: This rule does not apply to school teams.) A vacation request, signed by a parent, must be handed in 2 weeks before you plan to go on vacation. Failure to do this will result in your being dropped from the roster by the league office.

- During games, we stay together at all times. WE ARE A TEAM. WE ARE THE TIGERS. You can meet with friends on other teams after the coaches let you go home for the day.

- All players cheer on your fellow players. When a **Tiger** is batting, our bench is cheering loudly. Anytime you are on the bench, you are watching the game, cheering on your teammates, and listening to what the coaches are saying to other players. THESE ARE IMPORTANT CONTRIBUTIONS TO PLAYING BETTER AND WINNING!

- You are not a weatherman, and your parents are not weathermen. We will call you if a practice or a game is canceled because of weather. DO NOT ASSUME ANYTHING IS CANCELED. We love to use the telephone.

- No foul or obscene language will be used in any way. No razzing of the other team, the coaches, or the umpires will be allowed. The coaches will handle all disputes with the umpires. Players do not approach umpires with disputes.

- You will show the same respect for the parents who are helping the team as you would your coaches. You must show respect to all fans.

- All players will respect and care for the team's equipment. These are the tools of our trade. They help us succeed. There will be a consequence for abusing our tools.

- *(For school teams)* No grade lower than a C is acceptable. A player who is carrying a D or F grade has 1 (one) week to improve that grade or else that player cannot play in the next game.

- *(For school teams)* If you have broken a school rule and received a punishment from school, you will also have a team consequence decided by your coach. This is automatic—no exception!

- *(For school teams)* Academics are your No. 1 priority—always. Even so, studying for tests is not an excuse for missing a practice or a game. Athletics teaches you how to use your time efficiently. You have more than enough time to study and become a successful student. If you are having a hard time juggling your studies and playing baseball, please see one of your coaches, and he or she will help you.

Signed:_____

(Player)

Signed:_____

(Parent)

Signed:_____

(Coach)

Rules Violations

Age	Consequence Level	Implementation
5–8 yrs	1) Time out	1) Stop the child from the behavior and move him to another part of the practice area. Duration = 5 minutes.
	2) Chore	2) Have the child pick up debris from the field. Duration = 5 minutes.
	3) Go home	3) For a serious offense, and after the child has received other conse quences and the behaviors have continued.
9–12 yrs	1) Time out	1) Sit the player down and remove him from the stimulation of others. Duration = 10 minutes.
	2) Chore	2) Pick up garbage, pull weeds, remove stones from the outfield. Possibly heavier chores than those for younger kids.
	3) Laps/push-ups/ etc.	3) Go easy at this age, but it's good to introduce it now to prepare for the next level. Good if level 2 is not effective.
	4) Go home	4) After repeated offenses that called for the above methods first.
	5) Loss of playing time or loss of starting position	5) Can start to introduce this starting position consequence at this age. May not be too powerful for immature players. With more mature players it may be very effective. Parental response and support may be important to its effectiveness.
	6) Removal from team	6) After repeated use of level 4 and with consultation with parents first.
13–15 yrs	1) Sit down	1) Use like the time-outs of earlier ages

2) Exercise or chore

2) Or both. Try either or both to see which is more effective for each player.

3) Loss of starting loss of playing time

3) Remember that these are most effective when applied soon after closer to the offense, but start to work better at this age.

4) Staying after practice

4) Older players lives get busy and demanding, so now this traditional method starts to be more effective. This consequence offers a good opportunity to counsel/teach/coach the disruptive player.

5) Go home

5) After repeated use of the above.

6) Removal from the team

6) After repeated use of level 4 and after consultation with parents.

16–18 yrs

1) Sit down

1) This is embarrassing to the older player and can be very effective.

2) Chore or exercise

2) Same as level 1, just one step higher up the ladder.

3) Loss of starting position

3) Teaches that good players approach the game seriously.

4) Loss of playing time

4) Same as level 3, only piles on more consequence for actions.

5) Suspension

5) It works for schools and it can work for you. Insist on a conference with parents before returning the player to the team.

6) Expulsion from the team

6) Call a meeting with parents and discuss recommendations for improvement. Ideally, leave the door open for the player's return *next* season. It is important that you stick to this consequence if you go to this level. Reversals can be disastrous for the team.

Adult Attitudes

As you can see from the preceding chart, you have many options for rules enforcement with today's players. We recommend that when you have to employ a consequence, you should also help to coach the player through the enforcement. Of course, many coaches conduct their practices by themselves and, as a result, find that discussing the player's behavior and the coach's response to it while supervising 15 other players may be impossible. If coaches want to maximize their effectiveness and the team's success, then they should give the player a phone call after practice and discuss the discipline they are using and the reasons for the consequence. This phone call can be particularly effective, because, chances are, the coach will also get an opportunity to talk with a parent; this conversation will help to reinforce the coach's discipline system.

Some coaches almost pride themselves on not being disciplinarians to their players. They use phrases such as "It's not my job to raise somebody else's kids" or "I'm not a cop." We have all heard and maybe even used these phrases. However, when a coach shies away from setting and enforcing rules, critical elements of team building are lost. Players respect coaches who are in control of the team. They feel that they will be treated fairly and that they are safe and in good hands. Incidentally, this point about discipline should not be taken lightly. Think about how a player feels when he or she has to stand back and watch another player misbehave. Although they often don't talk about it, many players feel threatened by the "delinquent" player.

RULES AND TEAM COHESION

Team rules, as well as the enforcement of those rules, are great builders of team cohesion and a total team concept. One of the big causes of the loss of the team concept is the lack of rules enforcement. The other big contributor to this loss is the lack of emphasis put on team togetherness. Coaches should look for activities that their team can take part in together. Some good team-building activities include holding team parties, attending ball games together, developing a team T-shirt or patch that the players can wear to school, hosting study nights, or having a movie night. It is noteworthy that team homework nights or study nights are great team builders and work most effectively for the junior high and high school players. But even with players who don't attend the same school, this is a neglected technique that works well. It teaches players that they can depend on each other and work together even when they are taking part in mundane tasks like schoolwork.

Adult Attitudes

Coaches can do many little things to help create a team concept, such as the following: keeping their players together as they walk to and from the field; starting and finishing drills together; and saying the players' names aloud frequently during practice and also having the players say each other's name aloud. A fun practice drill is to have fielders call out their name when they catch the ball and call out the name of the player they are throwing the ball to. It is amazing how many young players do not know the names of their teammates. Another great team builder is to have a team cheer before and after practices and games. One particularly good team-building cheer begins with everyone clapping. As the players clap, everyone calls out each teammate's name. After the name is announced, the coach leads the players in a loud "Yea!" The cheer ends with everyone shouting the team name and then a final "Yea!" Before a game, the coach can add a special affirmation for the game, such as VICTORY or WIN or GAME TIME or PLAY HARD!

Chapter 2

Getting Cooperation from Parents

Very few baseball books talk about dealing with the parents, the fans, and the other adults who play an integral part in the life of young baseball players. As a result, this area remains the black hole of coaching. Mention the word "parents" to a high school coach who used to be a marine drill sergeant, and you will get a reaction that is the equivalent in explosiveness to a nuclear bomb.

The truth is, coaches like parents. We *are* parents! We know that parents are not life-sucking, evil harbingers of destruction who are ready at any moment to ruin your coaching career. Parents are people like you and me. It's just that when baseball, or any sport, enters into their children's life, they seem to automatically become a member of one of several typical categories of adults. These categories are as follows:

- The Ex-Player Parent
- The Fantasy Ex-Player Parent
- The Know-It-All Parent
- The Team-Owner Parent
- The Absentee Parent
- The Smothering Parent
- The Indulgent Parent
- The Permissive Parent
- The Loud, Aggressive Parent
- The Intrusive Parent
- The Ideal Baseball Parent
- The Multicultural Parent

Let's take a closer look at each type of parent (or adult or guardian) and try to understand them. Only then will we advise coaches on how to relate to each type in the most effective way.

Getting Cooperation from Parents

Keep in mind that even though these categories are stereotyped, every coach can tell you that he or she has encountered one or several of these types of adults while coaching baseball. Stereotypes help us prepare for situations in life. Stereotyping is just another word for rehearsing scenarios. If you understand and prepare for possible situations, you will be better prepared to cope with them.

THE EX-PLAYER PARENT

One of the appeals of baseball is that so many of us played it in some form as we grew up. Unfortunately, this fact has also created adults who were all heroes of championship teams 20 years ago. The fact is, there are the true ex-athletes, and there are the pretend ex-athletes.

The true ex-athletes are those who have self-confidence, who had a career highlighted by their own accomplishments, and who understand the job of coaching. These ex-athletes generally step back and allow coaches to coach. Behind the scenes, they may coach their children, but that's OK. Typically, they don't conflict with your coaching.

The other group of ex-athletes are those who live vicariously through their child. They typically lack self-confidence, either had minor success in their careers or had aborted careers, or were hard to coach themselves. These adults can be very intrusive to your coaching. For example, we know of one parent who would flash pitching signals to his son as he pitched a game. These signals often were opposite those the head coach had given.

As a coach, you should handle the true ex-athletes much the same. For those who stand back and allow you to coach, yet may be coaching their child separately, we say let them coach. However, it is important to establish that their child will follow your coaching when they are at your practices and your games. The same boundaries need to be established with the ex-athlete coach who is sabotaging your coaching. In our example of the father signaling his son, if we were the head coaches of that team, we would set a rule that this father could not signal his son. If the father did not comply, then he would be asked to leave the game. If he still did not comply, the boy would have to be prohibited from pitching for us again. This decision amounts to punishing the child for the sins of the adult; often, however, you are left with no recourse.

Of course, the ex-athletes who hover over their children intimidate some of us. Establishing your authority as a coach is very important at the beginning of the season with these adults. You are the one who has the ultimate clout in this situation, as you coach this person's child. The ex-athlete's past accomplishments or glories do not allow him to cash in these chips to overrule or bully you into coaching differently than you normally would. Later in this chapter, we will provide tips on how to establish your authority with parents in a diplomatic and positive manner.

THE FANTASY EX-PLAYER PARENT

The other group of ex-jock adults is those who were phantom players on phantom teams—in other words, the pretend jocks. There are multitudes of these people. If one could believe all the stories adults tell of their youthful exploits, then every high school baseball team would have 500 players, each of whom won the big game in the last inning with two outs.

Many times, these groups of adults are know-it-alls who are loud and who brag. Often, with their boasting, they ruin their child's self-esteem because they present an ideal that their child just cannot reach.

This group can also be infectious. They can incite other adults to act the same way they do. Your job as coach is to keep these adults away from the players; don't be tempted to get them involved with the team as helpers, team parents, etc. The biggest mistake a coach can make is to allow these adults to help with the team, to believe that by doing so, they will make their life easier. In fact, this error in judgment most often comes back to haunt such coaches. As a rule, coaches should pick their own assistant coaches and their own parent team leaders (who will be described later) and should stick with them.

THE KNOW-IT-ALL PARENT

Know-it-all parents or adults can range from those who truly know a great deal about the game of baseball to those who know very little, except what they hear on sports talk shows. In either case, it is important to realize that knowing a little about baseball is far different from being able to coach it and teach it to young people. This is true of so many things in life. Take the example of teaching school: Try controlling 25 fidgety 13-year-olds while attempting to get through your lesson plan for the day! Yet, all parents have an opinion on how you should be teaching their children.

Getting Cooperation from Parents

Know-it-all parents will approach you every chance they get and advise you on how to run your practice, who should be playing which position, and what game strategies you should employ. It is important for you to stop this meddling before it gets out of hand. One strategy is to restrict parents from approaching you at practice. Parents can be invited to watch practices, but coaches should plan ahead and set up a parents' area for them to stay. Make it clear from the first practice that if they do not interfere with the practice, it is to the advantage of everyone. To make this clear, you must not be afraid to confront these adults, for it is this confrontation that will establish your authority over the team from the outset.

Coaches who don't establish their authority lose respect from their team immediately. As we mentioned in Chapter 1, young people watch adults like hawks seeking prey as we relate to other adults. Your team will see your interaction with their parents and relatives as your baptism under fire. If you cannot handle parents, how will you be able to handle the prima donna player, the cheater, the lazy player, or the crybaby, or even an injured player? If you cannot handle these situations, why should I play for you? And is it safe to play for you?

Handling these know-it-all adults is easier if the coach realizes why these adults do it. One common motive of these adults is to feel that they are a part of the team. Another common motive is that for many parents, this is their way of searching for a method to relate to their child.

In either case, the coach can successfully cope with these adults by providing parents with a variety of roles they can perform for the team. We would suggest that you coaches do this early in the season, specifically, during your initial practices.

Before you have your first practice with your new team, write down a variety of roles that parents and relatives can play. Write down as many as you can create. You may never need them, but this ounce of prevention is well worth your effort. Some suggested roles for adults include the following:

- *Equipment Leader:* cleans, repairs, and transports all of the equipment; this role can be shared between parents.

- *Attendance Leader:* checks attendance at practice and telephones those players who are absent; this is a huge help, as many practices are delayed or aborted because of poor attendance and the need to chase down players.

- *Field Leader:* cleans debris off the field, waters down the field, trims grass, marks foul lines, etc.; the coach should make sure that all of these duties are specific and explained in detail.

- *Strength Leader:* (a nicer term than "water boy") makes sure there is plenty of water during a practice, especially in warm weather; duties can and should extend to providing snacks that can be allowed during practice, such as energy bars, fruit, or other nutritious energy snacks.

- *Statistics Leader:* helps out considerably at practice by keeping track of how many times a drill is performed, how many at-bats each player has had, how many pitches a pitcher has thrown, etc.

By having other adults handle these responsibilities, coaches are able to concentrate more fully on teaching their players. In addition, these jobs help to empower adults as an important part of the team. Another benefit of these duties is that they keep the practice interesting for the parents. Watching a baseball practice can be very boring for parents who have to wait for their children so they can take them home. Furthermore, the players will appreciate the parents' involvement with their activity and, as a result, better bonding will occur between parents, siblings, and players.

An important reminder to coaches: It is important to acknowledge these parents often for their willingness to take on the responsibilities outlined by the coach. We would suggest calling out these parents' names in the end-of-practice players' cheer. The coach should thank them often for their important role in helping to make for a great practice. One especially nice gesture is to present these parents with a practice T-shirt or hat or some other team apparel as a thank-you.

THE TEAM-OWNER PARENT

Akin to the know-it-all parent is the team-owner parent. These are parents who offer financial support for the team. Most often, this much-appreciated financial support comes with a hidden price tag. These parents tend to walk around, acting like big-league team owners. Often, their financial support starts innocently enough, as the parents buy snacks for the team or purchase some small, but important piece of equipment. In time, these gifts become bigger and more expensive—and so can the interference that these parents cause.

Getting Cooperation from Parents

Our advice is that coaches think up a dream list of needs before the very first practice. They should make sure to emphasize to parents that this list is truly a "dream list" and that parents may volunteer to purchase some of the items if they so desire. Coaches should also make copies for every parent and make a rule that no one parent can provide more than two needs. Although coaches may not get every item on their dream list, many coaches have nonetheless been very successful without all of their material needs met. Giving parents the opportunity to help out by filling a wish list also lets them know that there is something they can do to help the team. The dream-list approach allows all the parents—not just one or two sets of parents—to have a sense of ownership with the team.

THE ABSENTEE PARENT

The parents who a coach never sees throughout a season can be just as much of a problem as the meddling parents. We call them absentee parents, and they can hurt your team a number of ways: by setting rules for their child that conflict with scheduled practices, by taking vacations at critical points in the development of the team, or by sabotaging the coach's efforts in a variety of other ways.

We advocate an old cliché: *Get every parent involved as much as you can!* There are a number of ways to do this. One such way is to hold parent meetings, at which, perhaps, a team sponsor can provide refreshments and an assistant coach can run a movie for the players and their siblings while the coach and the parents chat. Another way is to hand out a parent newsletter, an idea that can be both easy to carry out and successful in its objective. The coach can simply hand write a message of greeting to the parents and include in the message what he and the players worked on in practice that particular week. The coach can then include a dream list, as well as other news the parents would be interested in learning about. For somewhat of a personal touch, the coach might choose to write out one note in his own handwriting and then make copies of this handwritten note—enough copies so that each player can take home two copies. Coaches should have fun with this project, even come up with a witty title that's a play on the team name or the coach's name. The newsletter might also contain reminders of upcoming practices, games, and other league events. What follows is a sample newsletter about our mythical Tigers team:

Getting Cooperation from Parents

The Tiger Times!

Hi, Parents and Friends!

This week we are working on bunting. Have your player show you the bunting position at home. Have some fun shadow practicing it at home.

Reminder:

This Sunday we are practicing at St. Jerome's Gym. Please have each player bring an extra pair of thick socks. We are going to practice sliding on the gym floor. If you can join us, please do. It's a lot of fun to watch the kids during this drill.

Note:

We still need a parent/friend strength leader to help with water, sports drinks, snacks, etc. Please see Coach Hayward to set this up.

Remember, our first game is only two weeks away!

THE SMOTHERING PARENT

Parents who smother their children can easily sabotage your coaching by preventing their child from performing the practice tasks you assign. These parents can hamper your coaching in a number of ways, such as keeping their child from playing in inclement weather or from playing a position that the parents feel is harmful or not in the best interests of their child; not allowing their child to play with minor illnesses; or making excuses for their child. The smothering parent can be very stifling to the player and may also be a source of embarrassment for the player and the team.

This type of adult is most effectively coped with by establishing the parents' rules (discussed earlier in this chapter). Unfortunately, it is often the player who is caught in the middle between your rules and the parent's smothering style. Being strong as a coach is the best way you can prevent any sabotage from this type of parent. It is important to fight these battles early in the practice season. Remember, most parents want their child to play baseball. Establishing rules may not be as risky as you may think. At the end of this chapter, we provide a sample list of rules for parents and players. Coaches and parents should use this list as a model that can be altered and personalized.

THE INDULGENT PARENT

The indulgent parent is very similar to the smothering parent and can be handled in a similar way. Indulgent parents can sabotage your coaching by showering their child with material things. This practice will prove disruptive to the team morale if the player constantly receives the "best" equipment or is imbued with special privileges because his parents or relatives indulge him. If a player has to miss team meetings because he and his siblings are required to go on trips with their parents, or if a player has to leave games early because of parental activities, the coach must disallow those absences because they will take away from team cohesion. A team should be treated as one, and the best way to establish this oneness is to ensure that each player is equal and treated equal. This philosophy should carry over to treatment from outside adults as well as the coaches. Certainly, coaches cannot control every aspect of how parents treat their children; however, they can control how these children are treated as players while they are part of the team and as their parental treatment affects the team .

The best method to cope with these parents is close communication. Let these parents know that their behavior is taking away from the enjoyment and productivity of the other players. Most parents will understand and comply. If a parent will not comply on his or her own after you have communicated your concerns to them, then set a rule that specifies certain behaviors that are not allowed. Be specific. Name each behavior you feel takes away from the team concept you are trying to build. To make it less personal, you can use your newsletter to talk generally about these type of problems with parents.

THE PERMISSIVE PARENT

Permissive parents are just as problematic as these other parents. Their attitude of allowing their child great leeway to determine his own actions can create a child who has never respected adult rule making. As a consequence, when you as a coach try to establish discipline for these players, they simply don't understand how to respond. It is not that they refuse to respond or that they are defiant of your authority; rather, they are, by nature, immature by the conventional standards of adult society.

These players whose parents are overly permissive are some of the hardest to coach because they don't respond to commands easily. Your coaching may have to take on a re-parenting function. With these players, it is important to stick to definite boundaries and roles. Unfortunately, the parents of these players are typically indifferent to your rules, so both the team rules and the parents' rules mean very little to them. Rather than fight battles with them over these rules, you should concentrate on your relationship with the player in question. After all, these parents are permissive! They are most likely going to allow whatever the player wants. The reason it is wise for the coach to concentrate on strengthening his or her relationship with the child is that children often respond to a decisive adult positively. It is as if the young person is looking for rules and structure—and you are the one who knows what the rules and the structure are.

THE LOUD, AGGRESSIVE, INTRUSIVE PARENT

The loud, aggressive parent is the adult who is loud at both practices and games, and who generally has a loud, aggressive manner. These adults can be intimidating to the coach, because they are so overpowering and overbearing. Usually, the old adage applies here: Their bark is bigger than their bite. It takes a special skill to be able to ignore loud, aggressive behavior from an adult, particularly one who is older than you. In these instances, you should keep your focus on your players' needs and the good of the team. The best method to employ in handling the loud, aggressive adult is to ignore them. You should never engage these adults in similar loud, aggressive behavior, because that will only serve as a reinforcement or encouragement for this type of behavior. That type of response will also set a poor example for your players. We guarantee that if you allow or feed into loud, aggressive adult behavior, then your players will view it as acceptable behavior and will soon copy it.

A basic principle of psychology is that the best way to eliminate undesirable behaviors in another is to give no form of reinforcement to them. Negative reinforcement (matching the loud, aggressive behavior with some of your own) keeps these adults behaving in the manner they see as effective. Remember the old saying: He is just trying to get a rise out of you! Positive reinforcement of loud, aggressive behavior (doing what the loud adult is asking) also encourages this behavior to continue. The golden rule for handling these adults is "Ignore them." The best tack is to speak to them only when they are calm, quiet, and respectful. In this way, you have taught the adult how you want to be treated. We use this approach in our lives all the time. It should be no different for coaches.

Getting Cooperation from Parents

THE IDEAL BASEBALL PARENT

The ideal baseball parent is defined as one who is having fun feeling a part of his or her child's team, yet not living vicariously through the child or the team. These parents find that being at the games is enjoyable as a recreation, and they see practices as interactive. They know their role and recognize that the coaches and the players have theirs. They do not interfere with the coaching; rather, they support and reinforce the teaching of the coach. As an example, a parent who watches his child at practice can reinforce the lessons of that practice at home by helping their child learn and develop certain skills, such as maintaining the proper batting stance and pitching form.

The coach should encourage the ideal parent by announcing to the parents present at practice what were the main points of that practice (refer back to the use of coaching notes or a newsletter). Example: At the end of practice, the coach can announce to the parents: "Today we tried to work on fielding positions. It would be helpful to go over various situations with your player and see if they know what their role is. Thanks! See you Wednesday." It is such an empty experience for parents who come to practices to just pick up their child without even getting a hello from the coaches.

The ideal baseball parent stresses the fun and accomplishment of playing the game over the competitiveness of winning. This attitude is very difficult for the coach to translate to the parents. We are raised in a society that views winning as the most important goal of playing. It is hard to change the mind-set of many adults to one that understands that the most important thing for their child is to have a great time playing, as well as a great time learning how to play better, being with friends, and giving his or her physical and mental best. The exhilaration of giving your best, of pushing your body, is a feeling that is not equaled in other endeavors, outside the world of sports. The ideal parent takes satisfaction in this great achievement by their child, at any age.

THE MULTICULTURAL PARENT

Because baseball is an international sport, many players may have parents for whom English is their second language. For these parents, it is important that coaches maintain a balance between treating them like any other parent and giving the extra effort to being able to effectively communicate with them.

Coaches may want to take advantage of the following tips: (1) translate all communications into their language, (2) invite them *personally* to team events, because they may exclude themselves due to the language barrier, (3) pay special attention to any forms of exclusion they may feel, such as the other parents not sitting by them or including them in team activities.

Food is such a universal language. Coaches should invite the multicultural parent to bring ethnic foods for parents' snacks at games, a move that can start a tradition of all the parent-fans taking turns bringing special snacks. It can also increase attendance at your games.

When you include the parents by taking an aggressive approach to inclusion, the players feel so much better about being members of the team that they will be motivated to play harder. We guarantee it!

A LITTLE BIT OF PREVENTION GOES A LONG WAY

We have been emphasizing throughout this chapter that prevention is the key toward obtaining the best cooperation from parents. So many coaches just neglect pulling parents into a cooperative spirit. This failure takes away from the team success and always seems to come back to haunt the coach and the team in some manner.

Along with the tips for gaining parental cooperation that have already been mentioned in this chapter, several other methods are particularly effective and deserve to be singled out.

THE PARENT LETTER

We strongly advocate giving each parent or guardian of a player on your team an introductory letter. Whether you hold a parents' meeting or not, the parent letter is a useful tool.

The parent letter is both a letter of welcome and a statement of the rules of the team.

Coaches should feel free to copy and borrow the sample letter that follows. We suggest that you either mail this letter to the parents or send it home with your players. But, if you choose the latter method, you should make sure you give each youngster two copies. Have the players get one copy signed by their parent(s) and return it to you. In this way, you have increased the chances that the parents will actually see and read the letter.

SAMPLE PARENT LETTER

Dear Parents:

Welcome to the 1998 Tigers! My assistant coaches and I can't wait for the season to begin. I would like you all to be a very special part of our success. In this letter, I will tell you how.

Our first practice will be Monday, March 20, 1998, at 5:00 p.m. We will meet at St. Vincent's Gym. Promptness is essential. Players who are late will have a team consequence.

We will practice every Monday, Wednesday, Friday, and Saturday until our season starts. Our first game is April 16,1998. The league has not given me the schedule yet, but as soon as I get it, I will pass on a copy of it to each of you. Once I get the season schedule, I will make up a schedule for practices between our games. Yes, we will practice throughout the season.

I have a number of simple rules that I want you all to know. These rules have proven to insure a successful and fun season. Attached is the list of team rules. Please read it, sign a copy, and have your child return the signed copy to me. This way, I know you have seen these rules. I look forward to a great season with you and your player.

Thank you,

Head Coach Mayer

Tigers' Team Rules

You must have a parent call me if you are going to miss practice. Attendance will be taken at each practice.

If you do not attend practices, your playing time and position will be affected. I don't care if a less skilled player is playing before you or in a better position. I would rather trust the player who commits himself to practice than the player with all the talent in the world.

My assistants and I judge each player's abilities through our practices, not on what they did last year or their reputations. If your son or daughter wants a certain position, practice time is when they win that position. We will give any player a fair chance to play any position he or she wants, but each player has to work for that position.

We love our moms, dads, brothers, sisters, aunts, uncles, and friends, but please don't phone us or pull us aside to plead your children's case on what position they should play or how they should be playing their position. WE ARE THE COACHES. We love your help, and that's why I am including the sheet that lists the kind of help we need for the team. I call these positions TEAM LEADERS, because they are so important to our success. If you can be a TEAM LEADER , please let me know right away. If all positions are not filled by April 1st, I will be calling you for volunteers.

No player will swear at games or practices.

No teasing or name-calling at games or practices; we respect each other and our opponents.

No players will play if they are out of uniform.

Always come to games with your uniform clean.

We have practice tee shirts. Our practice uniform is your Tigers' tee shirt and your Tigers' hat. Baseball pants, sweat pants, or jeans are suggested for practices.

We always cheer our team on, when we are in the dugout. Coach Thompson will keep order in the dugout and lead you in our team cheers.

After each practice and each game, we have a short team meeting with just the coaches and the players. Parents, please stand back from this meeting. I will also have announcements for parents after this short team meeting.

Getting Cooperation from Parents

No player will disrespect the umpires, their teammates, or the opposing team and its coaches and fans.

If you come late to a game, you do not play. But, you will stay and support your team.

By league rules, you are allowed one week of vacation time. You must let me know two weeks in advance if you are going on vacation during our season.

The player's safety is always our first concern. If you are not being safe at practice, or if you are not following the rules, you will be sent home. No fighting!

If a practice or game is canceled, you will get a phone call from one of your coaches. No players or player's parents are authorized to cancel a game or practice. If you don't hear from us, show up!

We are going to have a great season, win or lose, with a lot of fun for everyone.

Your Coaches:

Coach John—phone number = 123-4567

Coach Steve—phone number = 890-1234

Coach Bill—phone number = 890-5678

We Need Adult Team Leaders!!

Parents, an important part of making the *Tigers* a successful team are our TEAM LEADERS. These are parents, relatives, or adult friends of the players who volunteer their time to make the baseball experience healthy and happy for all the youngsters on the team. The *Tigers* need TEAM LEADERS in the following areas (Each area can have more than one adult leader):

Equipment Leader

Organizes, cleans, and maintains the *Tigers'* equipment for practices and for games. Can help procure equipment the players need.

Grounds Leader

Helps care for and maintain the practice and game fields. Keeps the grounds safe for the players. Inspects the grounds for safety, before practices. Helps arrange practice facilities.

Strength Leader

Arranges for all snacks and beverages the players use during practices and games. Our players need fuel to play their best and stay strong. This is a very important leadership for our team. Duties include pre-game snacks, practice and game health beverages, after-practice and postgame snacks. If we lose, it won't be because we aren't healthy and adequately fueled for the game.

Statistical Leader

Keeps statistics for the team. Keeps score during the games. Maintains practice and game records. This leader keeps attendance, the calling tree, addresses, and other records.

Social Leader

This leader organizes the *Tigers'* social events. Team parties, parents' parties, the opening-game party, the end-of-the-year party, etc. The coaches suggest that the team have frequent gatherings throughout the season to promote team unity. Some suggestions include movie nights (baseball movies, of course!), pool parties, arcade nights, etc.

Transportation Leader

Arranges transportation to away games. Arranges transportation for players who can't make a practice or a game because they don't have a ride. We will not have absences because of transportation problems.

Fan Leader

Fan support (parental attendance) is essential for success. This leader calls parents to get them out to the games and uses creative techniques to get parents in the stands. This is the Bill Veeck of our team.

OTHER TEAM NEEDS

Awards

We need team awards for the end of the season. Let's be creative here. Some of the traditional awards can encourage competition among the teammates. Let's think of noncompetitive awards that reward effort and good spirit among the team players.

We have 14 players on the team, so let's create 14 different awards. The following are examples of awards we gave out last season:

- Most Improved Player

- Catch of the Year

- Funniest Play of the Year

- Loudest Go-Go Guy/Gal on the Team

- Hard Worker Award (We gave away 8 of these!)

- Gamer Award (These youngsters are always ready to play.)

- Team Leader Award (We gave away 5 last year.)

We are not stuck on giving out only one of these awards in each category. In an ideal season, there would be 14 Hard Worker Awards.

Equipment

We always need baseballs and bats. Plus, every year, at least two players don't have a safe glove. But please talk to us before buying any equipment. Not only do we know the right equipment to buy, but we also may know where to go to purchase discounted items.

We always need new batting helmets. We could use flip sunglasses for the outfielders.

Clothing

If we had a donor, it would be great to buy team jackets, extra team practice tee shirts, and practice sweat pants. These items not only increase team pride, but they also keep players involved and motivated to play.

Getting Cooperation from Parents

Team Flag or Banner

If anyone knows how to paint well, it would be great to have a team flag. I would love to fly our team flag during our practices and at the games. Young people rally around flags and banners.

Practice Space/Meeting and Party Sites

If you know of a place where the team can practice when the weather is bad, please let us know. If you can arrange for a personal connection, that would be great! Similarly, please let us know if you can host a team meeting or a team party.

Thanks,

Head Coach Mayer

THE PARENT MEETING

Ideally, it would be great to have several parent meetings each year, but it is often not practical to do so. Therefore, let's concentrate on the beginning-of-the-year meeting with parents.

Many coaches avoid a parent meeting because they have been led to believe that they will not get any cooperation from the parents. We feel that it is the job of the coaches to get this cooperation. Coaches should be creative in attracting parents to this meeting. They should offer an incentive for the parent or the player to be at the parent meeting. They can even make it mandatory that a player can't play unless his parent(s) attend the meeting. Another suggestion is to hold the meeting on the day of registration, when parents are sure to be there.

Some points you will want to get across to parents at this meeting are the importance of establishing team rules, soliciting team leaders, establishing communication with the parents, asking for team needs to be filled, and giving the parents your philosophy on coaching, practice, and playing.

Coaches can distribute written copies of team materials to the parents at this time, but should also remember to distribute these materials again, several times, throughout the year. People will not treat these materials like the Bible; they will lose them, file them away, or otherwise neglect them. Distributing materials several times increases your chances that the parents will read them. As with the parent letter, the may want to have the players ask their parents to sign a copy and then return it to the coach. This system works for the classroom, and it can work for you coaches, too.

WORKING WITH SPONSORS

An often-neglected area of discussion in coaching at all levels is handling the team sponsors. In Little League baseball, sponsorship is a given; but even in high school and college baseball, dealing with sponsors is a reality that a coach has to live with. In these upper levels of baseball (i.e., post–Little League), state high school associations and national collegiate associations set firm rules for your involvement with sponsors. You need to be intimately aware of these rules and follow them strictly. Not being aware of how to use sponsors can cost you both games and players.

In youth leagues, coaches should communicate frequently with sponsors and let them know what the coach's expectations are and what the sponsors can expect from sponsoring their team. The league usually sends out a letter of thanks for their sponsorship. In this letter, the league thanks the

Getting Cooperation from Parents

sponsors and tells them they will get a team trophy if the team finishes high enough in the standings. We suggest you review this letter and add your own thanks. You can also include the list of team needs and team leaders that was given to the parents. You never know—this may get you additional sponsorship. You should send the sponsor a schedule of your games, and even your practices. You should even invite the sponsor to a practice to speak to the team. It is a great learning device for the players to understand what it takes to field a team or to know that the name on the back of their jersey is a real person or company. You'll be surprised at how eager a sponsor will be to talk to the team and how receptive the players will be in return.

A good method to keep sponsors involved is to use a technique just like the quick and easy parent's note you may send home with the players. Every once in a while, you may want to send the same, or similar, note to the sponsor. These gestures of goodwill may surprise you by the return good-will they generate. Remember that sponsors are contributing to your team for a reason. It could be allegiance to the baseball program, the need to market their business, or the desire to do a favor for a player or the family of a player. Regardless of the motivation for the sponsorship, it is important for you to be attentive to the needs of the sponsor. You should ask the sponsor for the reasons behind his or her contribution and then address the sponsor's needs specifically throughout the year. At the very least, you should give your sponsors an end-of-the-year note describing the success during the past season, how their sponsorship benefited the team, and—very important—how the sponsors also benefited from their contribution. You should have all the team members sign the note and include a ball signed by each player, or even a hat. These mementos will become trophies to your sponsor, and this gesture will go a long way toward assuring future sponsorship.

Another key to using sponsors is to just ask. If you have special needs, don't be afraid to ask. Sponsors are often glad to be included in requests that benefit the team. After all the team's success also reflects positively on the sponsor.

When asking for help from a potential sponsor, coaches should remember to be diplomatic in their approach. Such an approach may begin with a general appeal for help that includes the sponsor as a matter of course. Keep in mind that you are including the sponsor, just as you do when you send a message to the parents. You should make the same appeal or phone call to the sponsor that you would make to the parent. Most important, you should strengthen the impact of your appeal by making sure you follow up on it.

Chapter 3
Organizing Practices

Baseball coaches today can't afford to just walk onto a practice field, throw some balls down, and let the players romp around throwing, catching, and picking up bats and swiping at baseballs. Baseball is just too hard a game to play.

The importance of practice in baseball has been undervalued in relation to other sports, a fact that is particularly evident when people talk about baseball played at the younger levels. Yet, most athletes and experts agree that baseball skills are some of the most difficult to learn. The goal of this chapter is to get the coach to think about practices and become organized toward practices. Striving to reach these two goals will not only increase the success of your team tremendously, but they will also save you an enormous amount of your own personal time and headaches.

The first step a coach should take in order to run a successful practice is to formulate a practice plan *before* the players show up for practice. What follows in this chapter is a format for such a plan. It is easy to follow and easy to complete. The intent here is not to make you Sparky Anderson, but, rather, to make your world easier. When you are coaching older players, you should give them a copy of your practice plan. This move will save you time as you lead your players through practice. *Keeping players constantly moving in practice is very important for coaches at every level.*

PRACTICE PLAN

DATE_____   PRACTICE TIME_____

LOCATION_____   WEATHER CONDITIONS_____

TIME	DRILL	NOTES
	Stretching + Warm-ups	
	Throwing	
	Base Running	

SPECIAL ANNOUNCEMENTS!!!

Notice that we have filled in three practice drills for you already. The reason is that we feel that these activities are so important to every practice that we wanted to emphasize them. They will be discussed further throughout this book.

The real beauty of the practice plan is that it enables you to get the most benefit out of a short period of time and limited resources. Just like any job or other endeavor, the more organized you are, the more productive you will be. Think of how this same principle works at your job. As you approach the task, ready to work right away, having your tools organized and on hand allows you to get to work and complete that work in the most efficient amount of time. It is the same here. The practice plan allows you to get going the moment that your practice time starts. This organization can be a huge advantage when practice fields or other facilities are at a premium.

THE PRACTICE

Always begin your practice with a period of stretching, regardless of the age group you are coaching. Since players should never stretch "cold" muscles, please follow the warm-up guidelines provided:

WARM-UPS

- Arms—With hands on sides, lift both arms together, forward to a chest height. Do five repetitions. Return arms to sides. Now, lift arms straight out to the sides and raise them to shoulder height. Do five repetitions. Return hands to the sides. Now raise arms backwards as high as they will go for five repetitions. Finally, lift arms to form a 90-degree angle and then rotate arms forward and back for five repetitions.

- Legs—Raise one leg forward for five repetitions, then the other leg for five repetitions. Next, raise one leg straight to the side for five repetitions, then switch and do the other leg for five repetitions. Finally, lift one leg slightly off the ground and do forward and backward circles with the leg. Switch to the other leg and do the same movements.

- Slow, short jog—Pick a target on the field and have the players run to it and back. Emphasize that this is a *slow* jog; players shouldn't sprint, even though they may want to.

At this point, the team is ready to stretch.

STRETCHES

- Reach for the sky—Stretch your arms over your head, lock your fingers over your head, and hold for a count of 20. (Coaches should instruct their players not to hold their breath as they do this stretch.)

- Shoulder circles—Hold your arms out at your sides and make small circles, as if you are flying. Do this for a count of 20, then change the direction of your circles for a count of 20.

- Torso twist—With legs shoulder-width apart and planted, twist your upper body to one side, then the other side. Do 10 repetitions. (Coaches should let their players use their bats for balance, if they have them handy.)

- Neck stretch—Move your head to the left side and hold for 20 seconds, then move to the right side and hold for 20 seconds. Next, let your head hang down, with your chin touching your chest for 20 seconds. (As players get older, this stretch is more effective if they take the hand that's on the side the head is bent toward and *gently* tug as the head stretches.)

- Toe touches—Cross your legs in front of you and try touching your toes. Hold this position as you try to touch your toes. Hold for a count of 10. Repeat.

- Thigh stretch—(Players stand close to each other.) Place your left hand on the right shoulder of the player next to you. Grab your right ankle with your right hand and pull your ankle up, toward your butt. Hold for a count of 15. Change position. Place your right hand on the left shoulder of the other player. Grab your left ankle with your left hand and pull your ankle up, toward your butt. Hold for a count of 15. (Since older players may not get enough of a stretch by just pulling up their ankles, the coach should instruct them to move their leg out farther so they can feel more of a pull.)

- Groin stretch—Take a wide stance, with your legs more than shoulder-width apart. Bend at one knee, keeping your hand on the top of that knee. Slowly bend and hold for a count of 3. Bend at the other knee and hold for a count of 3.

NOTES ON STRETCHING

- The stretches described in this chapter were chosen because they can be done while standing. The advantage is that these stretches and warm-ups can be done under any field conditions.

- Teenage players should hold their stretches longer than youngsters.

- Coaches should remind their players that their muscles should stretch—not bounce—during these exercises.

- Before a game, coaches should add some specific stretches for position players. Pitchers can work on their shoulders by repeating the shoulder stretches. They can also help to loosen their lower back and abdominal muscles by doing more repetitions. Catchers can add slow, deep squats in which their feet are pointed out to the sides. Infielders can add squats and repeat stretches that loosen their lower back. Outfielders can repeat the leg stretches and also add quick sprints.

We recommend that all players warm up vigorously before games. Teams suffer whenever players enter the game cold. Since most players get better as the game goes on, or are just better second-half players, coaches should make sure their players are always physically ready to play.

Leg Circles Warm-up

Organizing Practices

Front Arm Warm-up

Side Arm Warm-up

Back Arm Warm-up

Front Leg Warm-up

90-Degree Arm Warm-up

Side Leg Warm-up

Organizing Practices

Touch the Sky Stretch

Shoulder Circles

Torso Twist with Bat

Neck Stretch

Neck Stretch with Hand Pull

Toe Touches

Thigh Stretch

Groin Stretch

Organizing Practices

After the stretching and warm-up session, the coach should assemble all the players and do a team cheer. The cheer doesn't have to be fancy, but it should be done by players from all age groups. The cheer provides great affirmation and serves as an excellent motivator. Both the coach and the players should have fun with it. The following is a sample team cheer:

Coach—WHO ARE WE?

Players—TIGERS!

Coach—WHAT DO WE DO?

Players—PRACTICE HARD!

Coach—WHAT DO WE DO?

Players—PLAY HARD!

Coach—WHAT DO WE DO?

Players—HAVE FUN!

Coach—HOW DO WE DO IT?

Players—TOGETHER!

Coach—WHAT DOES IT MEAN?

Players—WIN! WIN!

TIGERS!

TEAM!

You can use any cheer, or even make one up. The cheer should emphasize teamwork, fun, a goal (like winning), and practicing or playing hard, which means paying attention. You should also make sure every player is cheering loudly. Yell, "Louder!" when your players are yelling their part, but their volume is low. Repeat the cheer if the players seem lethargic. The cheer paired with the warm-up will get your team ready to practice with intensity. This is another reason why we stress the importance of keeping the players moving quickly through the practice: After the warm-up and the cheer, most players will be pumped up, so you don't want to have a practice at which they stand around most of the time.

PRACTICE TIME

Let's pause for a moment and emphasize an important point. Take a look at the amount of effort you and your team are already putting into team practices. Since you don't want this effort wasted, it is important to emphasize to the team the value of practice time. We do this in many ways besides just talking about it. If, for example, a player either misses practice or is late for practice, that player should suffer some team consequence (see Chapter 1). Furthermore, this consequence should be made very visible to the rest of the team. After all, the team is working hard. If a player is missing or late, he should be called up in front of the other players. By having him do so, you as the coach will be showing all your players that you will go out of your way to emphasize the importance of practice. If you get a parent on the phone, you should give them a mini-lecture on how important practice is and, again, let the other players hear your conversation. By acting this way, you are establishing your authority and, at the same time, teaching parents and players the importance of practice.

Many coaches aren't sure how many practices to have in proportion to the number of games their youngsters will play during the baseball season. Interestingly, here again, baseball has traditionally come up short compared to other sports. For example, it is not untypical for a youth baseball team to have no practices when it is playing two to three games each week—but that is a mistake. If your team plays two to three games a week, then you should be practicing three times a week. If your league schedules more games than this, say, three to four games, then you should practice twice a week. The successful team will be involved with baseball six days a week, with one day off. This diligence helps the players to learn and develop their skills, and it also promotes team unity.

WEATHER/INDOOR PRACTICES

One of the variables that your team will always be at the mercy of is the weather. Fortunately, your practices do not have to suffer simply because the weather conditions are poor. When the inclement weather forces you indoors, you can use your time wisely by working on strategy and game situations or showing your players how to use and respect the equipment. Another option is to watch films of baseball games with your players. At more advanced levels, you should watch films of your games, but when coaching youngsters, you should watch such events as college games or the Little League World Series.

Organizing Practices

You can also practice hitting form and fielding positioning indoors. This type of practice helps your players learn great muscle memory technique and is a valuable addition to your teaching. If you have the room, you can even do batting off the batting tee; fielding drills, such as rolling the ball (see discussion below); and even certain throwing drills, such as the one-knee drill (see discussion below). You can do many of these drills even in the typical basement, let alone a gym or a hall that may be available.

It's a good idea to ask your sponsor if he or she has some space available for practices on rainy days. By asking, you are getting the sponsor involved; besides, your sponsor may appreciate seeing your team in action.

Another rainy day tip that works well is to take your players outside at the end of the indoor practice and have them practice sliding in wet grass (without spikes, of course). It's easy, safe, and a lot of good, old-fashioned fun to be sliding around in the wet grass; however, you should wait until the end of the practice to do so, because the youngsters will be a mess afterward. If it is wet outside, but the rain has stopped, you can still throw the baseball around, even though you can't practice fielding or hitting (The ball gets too wet to hit or field). Practicing indoors or in bad weather will keep your team well disciplined and in rhythm.

PRACTICE: GENERAL NOTES

A good, solid practice should shape up like this: (1) Warm-ups and stretching, followed by throwing drills; (2) fielding drills in stations, once the players' arms are warmed up; (3) hitting in stations, then hitting as a team; (4) running drills. The following section breaks down each segment to illustrate how to get the most from each one.

WARM-UP REMINDERS

Warm-ups and stretching have been detailed earlier in this chapter, and you can use that as a guide. If you are going to substitute your own stretches or warm-ups, please keep in mind some general guidelines. First, you should get every major muscle group warmed up and truly get the players warmed up. Too often, coaches have their players do just a lazy jog to a fence pole and back as their warm-up. If you do that, you are setting yourself up for more work in the long run. Players who have not stretched or warmed up are the ones who have to sit out a portion of the practice because they don't feel well or something hurts them. When this happens, who is going to baby-sit these players?

THROWING PRACTICE

Throwing is one of the most neglected and undercoached skills in baseball, and teams pay dearly for this neglect. Therefore it is smart to include throwing in your practice every day. You should emphasize to your team that how a player throws in practice is how he or she will throw in a game—you simply should not accept lazy throws on the practice field. Do basketball players practice jump shots by flinging the ball at the basket with arms flailing? Of course not. Yet, when it comes to throwing the ball, you will see players at all levels throwing rainbows at each other with their arms in goofy positions and their heads turned around so they can look at the cute boy or girl from the other team. It doesn't look like a game of catch; it looks like a game of miss.

Since players are seldom in a position during a game where their throw is going to be only five to 10 feet, it's a good idea to have players throw longer distances in practice. The minimum distance from which to start your players throwing should be the distance between first and second base, as marked on a youth-league playing field.

You can help your players tremendously by teaching them to take pride in their throwing. A good throw to another player that is chest high and hits the glove is like a swish in basketball. As players throw, you should make a conscious effort to compliment them on their throws. You should refrain from letting your players toss the ball around behind your back, without any direction from you. Otherwise, they will think that throwing is not an important skill. If you take such a laissez-faire approach to throwing, then you will eventually create the situation in a game where a player's poor throw will cost you that game. If that happens, you really have no right to complain, because you have not shown that you care whether your players throw the ball properly. However, if you take pride in the art of throwing, your players will do the same—and they will win some ball games in the process.

On a team of 10-year-olds, we had a player whom we nicknamed "The Admiral." He threw the ball terribly. His hand and arm did some sort of contortion, and the ball went everywhere but the intended direction. The other players made fun of him. We worked with the Admiral every day, and his throwing improved tremendously to the point where we had confidence in his throwing and he played a great deal for us. But the most heartwarming incident came toward the end of the season, when the Admiral's mother came up to the coaches and told us how grateful she was for teaching her son to throw. She explained that her child had no father and that she knew nothing about baseball, that our work with him was like that of a father playing catch with his son. She said that all her son talked about at home was his coaches, who taught him how to throw the baseball.

A good practice habit to develop is to take part in 15 to 20 minutes of throwing drills. The throws should be chest high, line-drive types of throws instead of rainbow throws. To ease into the one-knee drill, the coach should have his players place the knee on their throwing-arm side on the ground and face the player they are throwing to. This maneuver teaches the players how to throw with their upper body. Before they drop to one knee, however, the coach should show them the proper form, which requires the players to hold the ball with their thumb under the ball and their fingers on top of the ball. The ball should be held up, with the players' wrist bending back away from the target. Their arm should be nice and loose, like spaghetti that's been cooked for 10 minutes. As the players release the ball, their knuckles should face the target. Their eyes should be focused only on the target.

Next, the players should stand up, with their feet positioned much wider than their shoulders. They are not to stride in this drill. They should, instead, simply throw to the other player, using a little rocking motion and concentrating on finishing their throw. Players should be taught to follow through with their arm (the spaghetti arm) so that their arm moves across their torso. They should exaggerate this motion during the drill, which we call the no-stride drill.

The players should then work on throwing and catching from an even greater distance. Again, they should start at the distance equivalent to that between first and second base. The players should stand in two lines, facing each other. They must catch with both hands during this drill. After they throw, the players should move back a step or two until they start to bounce the ball into each other. The players should make four or five more throws at their longest distance before they are finished with the drill. Again, the players should throw line drives to each other—not rainbows.

The One-Knee Drill for Throwing Practice

The No-Stride Drill for Throwing

During this last drill, coaches should introduce new skills. For example, this is a good time to introduce the crow-hop catch and throw. The crow-hop is done by catching the ball, balancing, taking a lead step that actually a quick hop, and then releasing the ball. The crow-hop gets more velocity on the throw.

At this time, coaches should introduce the concept of the relay player. The addition of the relay player will encourage the youngsters to keep throwing hard line drives with a purpose and also get them to thinking about the concept of the relay throw.

This drill also lends itself nicely to a practice game. The two players who end up the farthest away without bouncing the ball into one another should get a prize. For younger players, the coach should have some baseball cards handy to pass out. In short, coaches should do what teachers do. They should have gum, candy, small baseball items, or other little rewards in their coach's bag and let the players pick one out for "winning" the day's throwing drill.

The final throwing drill is the quick catch. After the last drill, the players are going to be positioned at their longest throwing distance. The coach should have the player who is at the farthest distance from the center of the practice area start to jog back in. As he comes jogging in, the coach should have him and his partner throw the ball quickly, catch it quickly, and then throw it back quickly until the two players meet.

This entire set of throwing drills should take only 15 to 20 minutes, yet it accomplishes quite a bit.

FIELDING PRACTICE

The put-out drill, which teaches fielding skills around the bases, is especially effective when it is done after the throwing drills. The coach should have the players line up in equal numbers at each base. Starting at home plate, the coach should have that player throw hard to third base. The player catching the ball at third base should step on the base and quickly throw the ball to the player at second base, who steps on the base and applies the tag to the imaginary runner. The fielder at second base then throws to the player at first base, who also steps on the base, tags, and throws back to home plate. The player at home plate who started this drill should have run to the end of the line at third base following his initial throw, while the player at third base should have run to second base, and so on. The coach should have the players complete one full round in this manner. When the player who started the drill at home plate is ready to throw to third, the coach should change the direction of the drill and have him throw to first base and continue the drill in the opposite direction for one full rotation. If any player commits an error, the coach should have him do it over again. This drill teaches the players to make tags and force-outs at each of the bases and how to handle pressure situations.

The next fielding drill calls for the players to form lines behind each other between third base and second base. The coach should have one player in each line come out of the line and stand facing the front of the line about half the distance between the lineup and the pitcher's mound. These players should roll a ball to the first player in the line. The roller should then run to the back of the line and wait his turn to be a fielder. The coach, meanwhile, should move from line to line and instruct the players on the proper fielding form. Occasionally, the coach should take the time to stop the drill and have all the players watch as the coach instructs them on proper body position and technique.

Granted, some coaches think that rolling the baseball is for the birds, that every ball should be hit hard and fast. However, the fact remains, you build confidence in players by having them succeed. A slow ball rolled to your fielders gives them confidence that they can field the grounder . In addition, they can also practice more easily the proper fielding form when they start out by fielding slow rollers. Coaches who try this method might be surprised at how much improvement their players make. Obviously, when they roll the ball, the players should not roll it at a speed that a turtle could beat out. The ball should have some speed to it, but the main objective should be to make sure your players feel comfortable fielding the ball.

The following fielding drills involve the practice technique that calls for the utilization of stations. The use of stations enables coaches to get their players involved in different drills at the same time. One way to take advantage of the situation is to divide your players into infielders and outfielders.

It is important to note that *all* your players should take both infield and outfield practice. You want players to be able to play as many positions as possible. Baseball teams always seem to be in the predicament of having to get by with players missing due to vacations, injuries, summer events, and other commitments, so practicing players at every position prepares the team for these emergencies.

In the outfield station, have your players form a line in the outfield grass. One player should stand with a coach. Have a coach hit balls to each player, in order, from left to right. After the players catch the ball, they should take the place of the player to the right of them. The last player on the right then takes the place of the player standing next to the coach. If the player makes an error, hit the ball to them over again. Have the players

Organizing Practices

throw the ball back to your "catcher" on one hop. The players should be practicing low, line-drive throws and also learning how to catch outfield hits. When the coach hits balls to the fielders, he should mix up the hits. Some should be line drives, some sky-high pop-ups, some short, some long, some grounders, etc. When each player has had a variety of different balls hit to him, conduct a bonus round. During the bonus round, the coach asks what type of hit the player wants to catch. It is interesting to see that most players want the super-high pop-up, as they have a lot of fun with that one. Their least favorite is the one-hop, line-drive hit in front of them. Pick out winners of the bonus round. Make it lively and talk it up while you hit the ball to the players. Ideally, if you have enough coaches helping, another coach could position himself with the players in the outfield and teach proper form and strategy while they wait their turn.

At the infield station, put players at the infield positions of catcher, third base, shortstop, second base, and first base. If you have reserves, have them stand in the shallow outfield to get the balls that make it through the infield. A coach should hit balls to each position and the players complete the play. To keep everyone alert in this drill, hit to positions in random order and again mix up the type of hit (i.e., grounders, fly balls, line drives, bunts). This is also a good time to yell out situations such as double plays. You can have even more fun by calling out triple plays.

The coach should rotate the infielders with the outfielders. At the beginning of the year, before the games start, these station drills will help you identify those players who are better at some positions than others. As the year progresses, continue to rotate the players through both infield and outfield stations. But, now, after all players have rotated between infield and outfield stations, have those players who will be infielders during games return to the infield station, and assign them to their game position. At this point, you should spend more time in these stations, because you are now building your position players. In this station setup, the coach can still rotate players to different positions to give them practice at other positions in case they need to be a replacement there sometime down the road.

This station drill for fielding gets much more practice accomplished for the entire team. It is a lot more productive than having the players stand around while someone is hitting the ball and hoping that it is hit to a player's position. This latter scene is often a coach's notion of a baseball practice: put nine players in their positions and have a batter step to the plate. This is a strategy that only serves to waste valuable practice time.

The fielding drill should take about 20 to 30 minutes. At this point, you have been practicing for about an hour and have accomplished a great deal with your time. Next, in our example practice, we can move on to hitting drills.

HITTING PRACTICE

Having a player hit for 15 swings before having him rotate into the field is not a productive use of hitting time. Here again, the station concept provides the best use of your time. Set up different hitting stations. A batting tee station has players paired together, with a batting tee lined up a few feet away from a fence or the batting cage. One player takes 10 swings, while the other player sets up the balls on the tee. The hitter is practicing perfect form (see the following explanation), and the tee is a great device to do this with. Many major league teams are using the batting tee for practices. Rod Carew, the batting coach of the Anaheim Angels and a Hall of Fame hitter, is a firm believer in using the batting tee at all ages.

Another station has a coach teaching bunting form. The coach is going through the stance and approach to the bunt first, then doing fast tosses to simulate bunting off the pitch.

A third station has a coach talking through and demonstrating perfect batting form with a batting tee. The coach then has the players take swings at the tee while the coach carefully watches their technique. This drill shows the coach how much the players are learning at practice. Using this drill throughout the year can be particularly helpful in detecting bad habits that invariably develop during a long season. It is a great learning drill for hitting.

Rotate every player through these stations once at each station.

Now, since the players are focused on hitting, we have them take part in a live pitching drill. In this drill, the ideal situation would be to have a player who can throw strikes pitch to the other players. Speed is not critical in this drill. In fact, tell your pitcher that you want strikes, but you also want him to save his arm by not throwing too hard. Again, going with the ideal, have your players assume their game-day positions and rotate the batter and the pitcher. As the players take 10 strikes, the coaches move around the field to instruct the fielders. One coach, the one who knows the most about hitting, stays by the batting cage and instructs each batter. That coach does not worry about the fielding. After each player has had 10 strikes, the drill is over. In the field, have the players complete all plays, but don't waste time

Organizing Practices

by having the batters run the bases. Some coaches we have seen have the batters run out their last hit (No. 10), but this wastes time and typically turns into a circus among the players. Although coaches do this to give the players base-running practice, that area can be dealt with later.

BASE RUNNING

The final activity for our sample practice is base running. Base running is another of those skills that are often ignored by coaches. Coaches assume that players know how to run around, so base running is not often emphasized in practice. There is a difference between running around and base running. We will devote a considerable amount of time on base running (see Chapter 6), so we won't go into detail now. Pick one of the drills in that section to employ at the end of practice. Use common sense here—base running drills are something you can do without much sunlight, so as your practices get later and later, save base running for last. And remember that base running is different than our warm-up. Just because a player has run, that doesn't mean you have *worked* on running.

SUMMARY

Now you have an efficient practice that takes up about two hours of time. The practice plan we have filled out on this sample practice appears on the next page. We have even mocked up some special announcements so you can see how to use that space on your practice plan. These are just samples of things you can do with your time. We strongly suggest that you change your practices frequently. Substitute drills frequently. Mixing drills up not only teaches new skills but also makes it interesting for the players. Occasionally, ask the players what they want to work on. If they are silly about this request, use their response as a way to teach them about working hard to become better and not just taking the easy way out.

Practice Plan (Sample)

Date___March 25, 1999_____
PracticeTime_____4:00pm_____

Location_____ **Weather Conditions**_ 55 degrees (and dry)_____

Time	Drill	Notes
4:00pm	Warm-ups	Shoulder-neck-leg stretches Jog around bases 2 times
4:15pm	Throwing Drills	One-Knee Drill/Standing Drill Long Catch/ Crow-hop/Quick Catch
4:30pm	Fielding Drills	Put-Out Drill/Grounder Drill Infield + Outfield Stations Game Positions + Stations
5:00pm	Hitting	Batting Stations = Tee/Bunting/Form Live Pitching
5:45pm	Base Running	Tags/ Base Sprints/Rounding

Special Announcements!!!

Uniform pickup is Saturday, March 30. Second parents' night is on that same evening, right after the close of uniform pickup. Pizza and pop will be provided by our sponsor!

PRACTICE GAMES

We mentioned the importance of changing the practice plan frequently to keep players interested, motivated, and having fun at practice, and all the while learning new skills. Practice games are a great way to shake things up, learn new skills, and have fun. Be creative and think up your own games or games coaches played with you over the years. Here are some suggestions:

- Long throws—Place a batting helmet on home plate. Challenge the players to hit the helmet from the outfield. The winner gets a prize. It would be especially fun to use the helmet of your upcoming opponent or your biggest rival.

- Pressure—During outfield drills, hit deep fly balls and tell players they will get a special privilege or reward if they go through one round with no errors. By doing so, you will force your weakest players to field and throw a ball perfectly under pressure. The other players will put pressure on the weaker fielders to do well so everyone can be rewarded. This game really works well and pays off in live games.

- Quarters—Players have to pay for errors, and the money goes into the team fund for a party at the end of the season. Don't do this every day, but declare certain practice days as "quarter days." Don't be surprised if the players ask for these days themselves.

- Home run derby—Hold your own home run derby. Each player gets 10 pitches and can count a single as one point, a double as two points, a triple as three points, and a home run as four points. The player who earns the most points gets a prize.

- Target throws—Have the players make medium- to long-range throws to a partner. Score one point for a throw that is caught around the head and at shoulder height, two points for a throw caught chest high, and zero points for a throw below the waist. An error results in the deduction of one point.

These are just a few suggestions of games that can perk up a practice. They teach concentration and how to handle pressure situations; they also reinforce basic skills.

Chapter 4
Building Defensive Skills

As we have mentioned earlier, baseball is a game of anticipation. This fact is magnified in fielding and defense. Your fielders should always be on the balls of their feet and ready to catch the ball. To help the players get ready to field the ball, the coach should instill in them a desire for the ball at all times. This aggressiveness is what makes great fielders. Those players who avoid making the play usually hesitate because they have been overly criticized for making errors. Therefore, you should teach your team that errors are a sign of aggressive fielding, and aggressive fielding is the key to becoming a great fielder.

INFIELD FORM

The perfect form for infield fielding is to approach the ball from the outside. If you do that, you will be in the best position to make the throw. On ground balls, the fielders should have the glove in front of them and the back of their hand just a fraction of an inch from the ground. The grass or dirt should just about tickle the knuckles. The players should catch ground balls with their legs—not their back. They should not bend their back; instead, their back should be held in almost the upright position. When the ball arrives toward the glove, it should be "received" by the glove by pulling the glove backward in a reverse scooping motion, as if the ball is fragile, like an egg. The heel of the throwing (non-gloved) hand should be placed on the heel of the glove, thus forming a trap between the two hands. As the ball enters the glove, the throwing hand should shut down on the gloved hand and close the trap. Some coaches have called this trap technique the "dust-pan pickup"—the player is closing the dustpan on the ball. Just before they make the catch, the fielders should step toward the ball with their right foot (for right-handed players) and then, at the last second, switch and step with their left foot. Their feet should be balanced or, at the very least, they should have a little more weight on their right foot. They should then be ready to throw properly.

The ready position for infielders is on their toes, knees slightly bent, back straight, glove held with palm up and low to the ground (some players "sweep" the ground with their glove). Their feet should be creeping forward as the pitcher goes into his motion to deliver the pitch to the plate. This position is the optimal position for the infielder to be ready to make any play.

Building Defensive Skills

Infielder's Ready Position

Scooping up a Grounder   **The Trap, or Dustpan**

The Infield Position—on the Balls of Your Feet

Fielding a Ground Ball—Approaching It from the Outside of the Ball

FLY BALLS AND OUTFIELDERS

When catching a fly ball or a line drive, the tip of the glove should be held slightly in front and just below the left eye for right-handed players (who represent the majority of players) and just in front and below the right eye for left-handed players.

As the fly ball comes toward the player, either outfielder or infielder, the non-gloved, throwing hand is positioned so that the thumb of the bare hand is touching the thumb of the glove. So now your trap is more on the side rather than straight up and down, as it is when you catch a ground ball. But the next step is the same. As the ball enters the glove, the bare hand closes this trap on the ball. Perfect!

The ready position for an outfielder is on the balls of your feet with your legs slightly bent. Both the glove and the throwing hand are resting on your lower thighs, and you are ready to run to the ball. As the pitcher is releasing the pitch, the players should be anticipating that the ball *will* be hit to them on every play—the optimum alertness. The outfielder's attitude should be: "I own this land. Nothing gets by me." Similarly, a coach can possibly accept a ball hit so hard it goes over the outfielder's head. However, if the ball drops in front of the player, then the coach knows there was a lapse in hustle, aggressiveness, or alertness.

The Outfielder's Ready Position

Catching a Line Drive or a Fly Ball

RULES FOR FIELDERS

As you teach your players fielding, keep in mind some traditional rules of fielding that are keys to success:

- The center fielder is the captain of the outfield. The center fielder takes precedence over the other fielders and can call the other fielders off a play.

- The shortstop is the captain of the infielders. The shortstop can call off other infielders on an infield play.

- Outfielders have precedence over infielders and can call infielders off plays.

- On a pop foul between the third baseman and the catcher, the third baseman has priority on the play.

- On a pop foul between the first baseman and the catcher, the first baseman has priority on the play.

- On a foul ball behind the first baseman, the second baseman usually has a better angle on the play than a backpedaling first baseman.

- The pitcher should think like a fifth infielder and not be passive on the field.

- Teach players to go after all balls unless called off by the position player who has priority (such as those outlined here).

- When two infielders are on a sure collision course, the pitcher should call off one player by calling out the position of the player who should make the play. The pitcher may have to physically stop one player from colliding into the other.

In general, for all defensive positions, teach your fielders to be thinking that "I'm going to make the next play, and that play will be to my left or to my right, behind me or in front of me, but not right at me." This focus keeps fielders in the best state of alertness on the field.

SPECIAL CONSIDERATIONS FOR SPECIAL DEFENSIVE POSITIONS

Catcher

We've talked about the center fielder as the captain of the outfield and the shortstop as the captain of the infield. Given these rules then, the catcher should be seen as the overall field general. Catcher is such an important position, it deserves special consideration.

Use the catcher to determine where the relay throw will go. Have the catcher yell out "1-1-1" (for the throw to go to first base); "2-2-2" (for the throw to go to second base); "3-3-3" (for the throw to go to third base); and "Relay-Relay-Relay" (for the throw to go to home plate).

The coach should go over these situations with the catcher during practice. He should instruct the catcher on what throw to make during certain situations. We recommend that you single out your catchers and go over these situations individually, making sure they understand their role.

Other practice drills to do with catchers individually include the following: rehearsing good catching form in the squat; throwing balls in the dirt to practice blocking the plate; throwing to second base and throwing out the stealing runner; going after pop-ups; practicing the bunt situation; tagging a runner out at home plate; and learning how to "frame the plate" for the pitcher.

Let's take a closer look at a few of these skills for a catcher to master. When teaching the young catcher to go after a pop-up or to throw to second on a steal try, teach the player to keep the catcher's mask on. Young catchers waste a good deal of time and often confuse themselves by trying to coordinate ripping the mask off, handling the catch, and then throwing the ball or chasing the foul ball. If your catchers complain that they cannot sight the ball on these plays, then how can they catch the pitcher's throws so consistently? Similarly, when the play is to tag out a runner at the plate, teach your young catchers to keep their masks on for safety.

Framing the plate is an advanced skill for catchers. It is a great help to your pitchers, and it involves several motions. As the pitcher is setting his sights on the plate, the catcher "frames" the strike zone slowly by outlining an imaginary square. The other motion involved in framing is for the catcher to pull, or frame, the ball into the strike zone as he catches a pitch just off the strike zone. This motion should be quick; and the swifter the motion, the better the chance of pulling the ball into the strike zone.

On bunts, teach your catchers concentrate on getting the lead runner, unless told otherwise by the shortstop or the pitcher. This focus prevents the catcher from hesitating.

A good bunt drill for your catchers is to have players line up behind the catcher. A coach rolls a ball (like a good bunt) in front of the plate. The runners then run to first base as the catcher practices the pickup and throw to first.

Other Defensive Positions

The first baseman should assume a position around the mound on hits that go far past the outfielders. This is particularly important on fields with no fences and with younger players who can't make the long relay throws to home.

The second baseman is the relay player for deep hits to right and right-center. A good second baseman is very active and moves freely around his position.

The shortstop is the captain of infield pop-ups. The shortstop should have the strongest arm of your infielders. The shortstop is the cutoff player for the left fielder.

The left fielder should be instructed not to hug the third-base line. The coach should prefer to have a foul ball drop than to have the fly to left-center fall in for a big hit. The left fielder needs to back up all plays to third base.

Building Defensive Skills

The center fielder should be the fastest of your outfielders. The center fielder backs up plays to second base.

The right fielder should have the strongest or second-strongest arm on the team. Many coaches put a weaker player in right field, and this is a strategy that usually backfires. At younger ages, hitters swing late, and the right fielder is a busy player. Further, the fly ball to right field to advance or score a runner is the oldest offensive strategy in baseball. This fielder has to catch well and have a good arm. The right fielder backs up all plays at first.

The pitcher should back up all ground balls by taking up a position in the field where the ball could go through on the throw to a base.

CHOOSING A GLOVE

Let's pause a moment and consider the tool of the fielder's trade—his glove. When choosing a glove for youngsters, it is a good idea to concentrate on getting a good-quality glove and one that fits comfortably.

When players start to develop, parents and coaches can then start to worry about whether they should choose an outfielder's glove (usually a bit longer in the fingers) or an infielder's glove (usually a bit smaller in the fingers). It is only when players begin to define their positions that you will want to make this differentiation.

Players will ask about breaking in a glove and how a glove should feel. As a general rule, an infielder's glove should be broken in to stay more open and an outfielder's glove should be broken in to stay more closed. The Stan-Mil Fielding Mitt is an effective glove insert that resembles a batting glove. It helps get more life out of tired, floppy gloves, and it has the extra physical and psychological benefit of giving younger players more confidence about fielding because it helps take the sting out of catching a hard ball. Have younger players try this fielding glove insert, and you may see a big differ-ence in their defensive confidence.

PRACTICING FIELDING SITUATIONS

A valuable practice technique to use to practice defense is to go over situa-tions that mimic game situations. In this section, we would like to go over some valuable situations that should help your game preparation.

Before going into specific plays or situations, you should consider some general defensive points: Teach players to talk to each other when on defense. Too few players talk to the other fielders. Calling for balls, informing other players of the offense's tendencies, reminding each other who has the cutoff or the coverage on a base, and relaying the coach's instructions are all valuable defensive tools. At practice, go over clear and loud communication between players—truly practice game situations.

Situation Drill: Tell your players there are no outs, it is the last inning, and your team is up by one run. Put runners on second and third. Hit a fly ball to center field. Teach the team that the throw from the center fielder goes to third base if the ball is hit deep. This strategy should prevent the winning run from advancing to third base.

Again, use this same setup, but this time, practice what should happen on a ground ball. Have your catcher call out where the play goes. Remember, the catcher is the field general. Next, practice on a ground ball that goes through for a hit. Where does that throw go?

Other situation drills you should put the players through are the various relays that will need to be developed. You should practice relays from left field, right field, and center field.

The key to practicing defensive situations is to use your imagination as a coach. Imagine situations you have seen or been involved in and then run your team through the situation many times. Obviously, the more familiar your players are with a certain situation, the better they will execute it in a game.

Chapter 5
Fundamentals of Hitting

THE HITTING STANCE

As they get into their stance in the batter's box, players should keep their legs shoulder-length apart. The stance should be an athletic stance that is strong and balanced. The players should be on their toes, with their knees slightly bent. To explain this stance to the players, tell them that the stance is the same as one taken when guarding someone in basketball or when blocking in football. A coach can test the strength and balance of each player's stance by giving the player a slight shove on the chest while he is in his hitting stance. If the player holds his position after the shove, then he has the proper balance. If the player flops around, losing his balance at even a slight shove, then he is not strong and balanced. Coaches should do the balance test with their players frequently. They should see a big difference in their players' power when the players are in the proper stance.

LEG POSITION

Once the stance is mastered, the toes should be pointing in toward home plate, with the knees inside of the feet. Weight should be shifted more to the back leg. The ratio of weight between the back and front legs should be 60-40, with more weight shifted to the back leg.

Fundamentals of Hitting

The Hitting Stance

Checking Hitter's Balance

Foot Position/Knees Inside

Initial Weight Balance

The hitter should stand tall. The back knee should go forward into the ball, just like on a throw. As the hitter drives forward, his shoelaces go up into the ball. On contact with the ball, the shoelaces face the ball, while the hitter's knee, thigh, and buttocks are going up into the ball. The result is that the back foot ends up on its toe when the hitter is making contact and the power shifts to the front leg. This position provides the most power. The quicker the back knee drives to the ball, the quicker the hitter's hands will be.

HIP MOVEMENT AND "SQUISH THE BUG"—STOP!

It is hoped that, with the popularity of the movies *Antz* and *A Bug's Life*, young players will let those poor bugs live. All kidding aside, a popular way to teach hitting to young players has been this technique of "squishing the bug." In that technique, you teach the player that the hip needs to move on contact with the ball, and that, in order to move the hip, the player must grind the ball of his back foot into the ground, as though he is squishing a bug with it.

Unfortunately, squishing the bug does not teach players to *drive* their legs and hips through the ball. The result is that they are not being taught to get more power into their swing. Squishing the bug is, at best, a weaker way to make contact and, at worst, distracting to young players. Instead, the coach should instruct them on the importance of driving the ball and generating power on contact.

Many coaches can be heard nagging players about hip movement. Our approach de-emphasizes the hips. Everything that you need to know about hip movement will be taken care of if you teach good back-leg movement, extension, and follow-through in the swing. Overemphasizing the hips at a young age will result in players pulling away and spinning off the ball.

Fundamentals of Hitting

Driving Forward   **Contact**

Driving through the Ball   **Stride—Really a Reach!**

THE STRIDE—REALLY A REACH

In recent years, many South American players have been taught not to stride during their swing. In most areas of the United States, players are taught to stride into the ball. Our approach advocates teaching players to stride when hitting. However, it is important to note that your players may see successful Latin players on television or at the games who do not stride. Your players may want to copy that style. At the very least, they may cause a commotion at practice by imitating the no-stride approach. To help their players learn the proper fundamentals at a young age, coaches should tell their players that if they continue on with baseball at the high school or college level, most coaches will be looking for a stride in their swing.

The stride is a more delicate maneuver than many young players are used to executing. It really amounts to a reach with the front leg. If the player has been adopting a good stance, as detailed here, then his front foot should begin with less weight on it than the back foot and leg by a ratio of about 40-60. The hitter is then lighter on his front foot when he begins his swing. With the weight on his back leg/foot, the hitter will want to take a reach, or a stride, with his lighter front foot for about a few inches, just before the ball arrives at the plate. The hitter should land on the inside of his big toe. Landing on the inside of the big toe will help him shift to the 40-60 weight balance that adds power to the contact. This begins the process of weight transfer and the addition of power to the contact with the ball.

An easy but effective drill to have the players do is the Stride Drill. Just have them line up with their bats on their shoulders. Give them a command of "Stand—Stride." Do this over and over again until you see soft, well-balanced reaches, with their feet landing on the inside of their big toe.

Fundamentals of Hitting

Reaching and Landing on the Big Toe

Shoulder down and toward the Ball

SHOULDER POSITION

The front shoulder should stay closed—arm toward body and shoulder down—and the farther away from the plate it is held, the longer it will stay closed. This is a big key in hitting. The hitter should have his front shoulder go down toward the ball and stay there. The longer the player can keep that shoulder closed and throw a "punch" from the back with his back shoulder driving the punch into the ball, the more successful the hit will be.

HANDS

You may have heard the term "quick hands." In actuality, it's not quick hands as much as it is "quick bat." If the player is putting together all of the motions that are outlined in this chapter—and doing it quickly and with precision—then his bat will swing like a bullwhip toward the ball. The faster the bat, the harder the ball will be hit. It doesn't take massive muscle to hit the ball hard—it takes great bat speed. Just ask Ernie Banks, Hank Aaron, or Willie Mays. These were not giants of men, but they were power hitters in baseball because they had tremendously fast bats. What you want to emphasize with the players is that their hands move through the ball so that the bat moves right through the ball.

The hands should stay back about an inch or two from the body. The punch that the hitter throws to the ball is a straight line to the point of contact—no roundhouse punches or uppercuts. The greatest amount of energy is delivered by a straight-line punch. In other words, the player is not really swinging at the ball, but rather punching at it.

HEAD/EYES

The eyes should always be forward as the pitcher is winding up. The hitter should then follow the ball all the way into the plate. The ball is all that is looked at during hitting. The head should have the least amount of movement of any body part during the swing. The less movement by the head, the better. The head should also be in a lowered or down position. The more the head is down during the swing, the more the hitter will be able to swing through the ball.

As the hitter is looking forward at the pitcher delivering the ball, his chin should be resting on his front shoulder. As the hitter keeps his head still, and as his shoulders move through the swing, his chin will automatically shift to a resting place on his back shoulder. This change is not done by the chin itself, but by the movement of the shoulders. Watch carefully for your players to keep their heads down and still as they practice. You can help them out by putting down a ball or some other marker on the outside corner of home plate. As the player practices off a tee or in flips, instruct him to end up with his eyes looking at the marker.

Fundamentals of Hitting

Head Position Down

Chin Shifts to Back Shoulder

Weight Shifts to Front

The Follow-Through

THE FOLLOW-THROUGH

As the hitter's head stays down and still, he should let the bat follow through the swing. His front foot at this time should have landed on the ball of the foot inside of the big toe, and the weight has transferred to the front leg to a ratio of close to 70-30 or more.

Teach the players in the follow-through that not only should the body's weight be on the front leg, but also the entire body should be pushing forward. This slightly off-balance lean not only means that the energy of the swing has been properly transferred to the ball, but also that it puts the player (a right-hander) in a great position to run to first base.

THE MENTAL GAME OF HITTING

The mental approach to hitting is as important as the mechanics that are detailed here. Many experts over the years have called hitting the baseball the single most difficult task in any sport. In earlier chapters, we have discussed the high failure rate that is part of baseball—especially when it comes to hitting. But that doesn't mean that hitting should be approached as an impossible task. Our mental approach can redefine success and should redefine success for the young player, T-ball through high school.

As their coach, you should build confidence in your hitters. Don't pressure them into getting hits. Many coaches think they are motivating players by yelling, "Come on, ya got to hit this one!" or "Why didn't you swing at that? You can hit those!" or "Come on, you're better than that!" These statements do not constitute encouragement. They more closely resemble nagging. Does a basketball coach yell, "Come on, ya gotta make this one!" to the player at the free throw line? No, it's as quiet as a church when a player goes to the line. If the coach speaks to the player at all, he offers words of encouragement, such as "Do it just like in practice, Jamie."

During one crucial moment in a playoff game, one of the authors of this book went up to a player who was about to bat with runners on base and a chance to take the lead in a tight game and said, "Listen, Ben, after you get your hit, look at me right away because I might just send you to second on their throw home."

The coach had no grand plan to do that, but he wanted the hitter to relax and think positive, yet not be thinking of a pressure hit like a home run. The result was a solid base hit, and the player did make a double out of it.

Fundamentals of Hitting

Your statements to your players are vitally important in establishing the right mental attitude toward hitting. Try hard not to get down on them for their mistakes and encourage the players to succeed. After all, your players are the ones up there performing—and not you. For example, if a player takes a swing at a pitch over his head with no strikes on him, we might say, "OK, you had your fun now. That was way over your head. You've got two more strikes to look at. That-a-way, let's git the next one! Let's go! Stay in there. Look at the ball." That is so much different and more productive than the negative "Hey, what are you swinging at? Are you blind? Come on, you know better than that. Only swing at strikes!"

You start building hitting confidence at practice. Let the players hit the ball during practice. Doesn't that seem to make incredible sense. Yet, at so many practices, coaches will have their best pitcher throwing batting practice, and that pitcher is trying to impress everybody by throwing hard and fast to the batters. This strategy does not build confidence in your hitters. Either tell your pitchers to pitch slow and easy or have an adult coach pitch batting practice. The advantage to having a player pitch the batting practice is that you can then stand by the batting cage and teach hitting, while the player who is pitching gets a chance to practice fielding the pitcher's position.

CHOOSING YOUR WEAPON (BAT)

Many parents of young players don't know how to pick the best bat for their child. Like the young players themselves, and maybe in response to the young players' wishes, parents feel that the heavier the bat, the better the hitter. False! As we have been emphasizing throughout this chapter, good hits are a product of bat speed—not heavy clubs. To help your players achieve fast bat speed, you should be using and thinking lighter bats. Don't go for heavy bats at young ages.

There is a simple test that will help you determine the right bat for each player. For a right-handed hitter, stand with the player a good distance from you, with right side facing right side to the point where you can barely shake hands. With your arms extended straight out from your body, take the player's hand in a shake, withdraw your hand, and replace it with the grip end of a sample bat. With the player still standing to the side with his arm straight out, the player should be able to hold that bat straight for five seconds. If the bat tilts downward, it's too heavy. If the player can hold it longer than 10 seconds, it may be too light.

THE GRIP

The proper way to grip the bat is to place the hands together with the knuckles lining up with each other. If your players are not generating enough speed with the bat, try having them move their hands up on the stem of the bat, or choke up on the bat. There is no science to choking up. It is a feel by the player or an observation by a coach. Have a player try it, and if it feels better to the player, encourage the player to keep this grip. One other tip here: You have to keep reminding players to choke up until it becomes a habit of theirs.

The Bat Shake to Size up the Right Bat for a Player

Fundamentals of Hitting

TO GLOVE OR NOT TO GLOVE

Batting gloves are a very useful tool for hitters. The batting glove gives young hitters a better grip on the bat, which allows them to keep their hands loose in the grip. Having a better grip also makes it safer because there will be fewer bats slipping away from hitters and flying into the field.

Batting gloves are designed differently. Most are just designed to have a better gripping surface, but some are padded to help absorb the shock or sting of the metal bats that youngsters these days use. The original padded glove—the Stan-Mil Mitt—is not only still the best, but it also has the added advantage of positioning the hands correctly. For serious players, the Stan-Mil Mitt is the one to have.

Finally, a batting glove gives hitters confidence. They will feel as if they have an extra tool to use to hit the ball better. Anything that gives the hitter a mind-set of more confidence can only help.

"The Grip"

Chapter 6
Coaching Base Running

COACHING BASE RUNNING

A neglected area of youth coaching is base running. This is puzzling for two reasons: (1) successful coaches at the upper levels all stress the importance of base running in winning games and (2) the younger the player, the more that base running is a huge part of scoring runs and winning games. At the youngest levels of baseball, games become parades of players rounding the bases on the heels of dribble hits. Yet, because base running is not properly taught, these games are chaotic. For example, you will typically see coaches yelling instructions at base runners and players starting and stopping in the base paths who are anxiously searching for their coach's attention to get further instructions. Yet, teaching good base running at younger ages builds such good habits. Thus it is imperative that coaches start teaching good base running skills at the earliest ages.

THE FIRST STEP

Let's break down base running into discrete elements and make it more effective. Better running to first base starts at the moment a batter is swinging. We discussed in the last chapter how the shift in the hitter's weight from back leg to front leg contributes to a lean toward first base. Thus, a better hitting stance immediately puts the player in position to get a better lead to first base. As the player moves toward first, there is nothing wrong with his taking a quick look at the hit, *as long as it is only a quick look*. The players should maintain the momentum they started during their swing and continue a lean toward first as they run. The players' toes should be pointed straight toward first base, and they should be pushing off their back leg as they burst out of the batter's box. We are big advocates of taking a straight-line run toward first base. Some players have a tendency to make wide, elliptical runs toward first, often running themselves out of the base path in the process. This happens because the leaning momentum after their swing angles them toward this outside route. You should teach your players to adjust their momentum so they can run a straighter path to first base.

PRACTICE DRILL: A good base-running drill is to flip a ball to a player while he is still in the batter's box and practice the start to first. Just have him make the start to first over and over while you are correcting his initial path, burst of speed, quick look, etc.

RUNNING TO FIRST

As the player approaches first base, he should hit the base with the front part of his foot and run through the base. Teach your players that they should run like as if they are going 10 feet past the base. The runner should look down quickly at the base, making sure he made contact and also that he doesn't trip over the first baseman's foot. The player should then immediately take a quick look at the first-base coach to get the coach's instructions.

As players run through the base, teach them to take a "banana curve." The banana curve is done by dropping the left shoulder and making the turn after running through the base, as if going to second base. Players need to realize that they cannot be thrown out on a base hit for running through the base. Some younger players appear hesitant after reaching first base. You must teach them that they are safe there, but that this rule for running past the bag does not apply to the other bases, except for home plate.

This banana curve accomplishes several things. On a base hit, it forces the outfielders to be alert; consequently, they may hurry their play. Hurrying the defense's plays increases the chances that an error will be made and that you may get to take an extra base. The banana curve also teaches the good base-running habit of always thinking one base ahead—the essence of aggressive base running. Finally, it makes a statement to the other team that you are going to be aggressive. Again, this makes them hurry defensively throughout the entire game.

If the base hit is longer than a single, and the player is sent by the first-base coach to second, the player should run to second base without looking at the location of the ball. The player should run, without searching for the ball, and should trust his coaches. Discipline and practice are the only ways to establish this habit.

This essential skill provides a perfect example of the hypocritical coach. This coach is one who doesn't practice this skill. Yet, during games, he will scream at players who pause while running the bases to get their own look at the ball.

Coaches, these are kids. If you want them to perform differently, you have to teach them. They don't learn through osmosis.

PRACTICE DRILL: To practice the banana curve and help players learn to trust their coaches, have the players run from a starting point five feet from the batter's box. A coach either hits the ball off a batting tee or just hits it out into play. The player then runs without looking at the ball and only taking instructions from the coaches. If they look at the ball at any time during the drill, then they have to stop immediately right there and go back to the start. Players will learn quickly to listen because they won't want to be sprinting over and over again.

The next step in better base running is to break down leadoffs, including getting the sign and stealing. Before taking a lead, the runner should be taught to take a quick look at the outfielder's position. In this way, the runner could gain an advantage on a hit into the outfield by knowing if a ball will fall in or get past the outfielders.

THE LEADOFF

A proper leadoff consists of taking three stutter or hop steps, always facing the pitcher as the body moves off the base. In this way, the runner is alert to a quick pickoff attempt by the pitcher. The runner at first should always have his eyes on the pitcher. As the pitcher releases the ball to the plate, the runner should immediately take two more quick stutter or hop steps toward second base. Ideally, the second step should be timed so that the player is landing with his left leg first, as the ball is at the contact point over the plate. In this way, the player is ready either to dig for second or to lunge back to first. During this time when the ball is approaching home plate, the runner's eyes should be focused only on the batter and the ball. The runner should stay alert to see if the ball is put into play. If the ball is hit, then the runner explodes toward second base. As the runner comes to about the halfway point between first and second base, he should take a quick look at the third-base coach to see if he is going to be waved on to third or instructed to hold at second. Again, the disciplined runner trusts the third base coach for signals and doesn't waste time by looking for the location of the ball.

STEALING

The steal is one of the most exciting plays in baseball; when done properly, it is also one of the most technically demanding. The steps needed to successfully steal start with the runner getting the sign from the third-base coach. Once the runner is given the steal sign, he should use one of the

Coaching Base Running

proven methods of gaining an advantage in stealing. Following the five-step stutter or hop-step technique described above certainly starts the runner off with an advantage. But most experts agree that runners will gain a huge advantage by watching the pitcher's heels. If the pitcher's back heel rises up off the rubber, he is going to throw to first. If the pitcher's front heel rises up off the rubber, then the pitcher is throwing home.

If the pitcher throws toward first for a pickoff and the throw is close, the runner should slide back to first by leading with his right hand extended. He should reach for the outfield side of first base and turn his face away from first base as he slides back. This not only gives the runner another advantage, but it is also a safety measure to prevent the runner from being kicked in the face or struck by the ball. Coaches should teach their base runners to keep their fingers loose as they lunge back to first. Stiff fingers get jammed and hurt.

Another strategy that deserves consideration is the runner's decision when the pitch is thrown in the dirt. The coach needs to assess the catcher's ability to throw quickly and accurately to second (or third). If the catcher has difficulty releasing quickly, then the runner should take the chance for an extra base when the pitch goes into the dirt. This is particularly true at younger ages, where, odds are, the catcher will not be fast enough to make the play to the base. If a coach is going to take this strategy in a game, then he should let his players know early in the game. It is a simple rule for players to follow: If the pitch is in the dirt, then automatically run to the next base

Lunging back to First—Head away from Base

Coaching Base Running

The Leadoff Stance

The Last Lead Step

The Lean out of the Batter's Box

The Banana Curve

Coaching Base Running

Indoor Sliding Practice with Socks

PRACTICE DRILL: Have the players take a position on each base. There is no batter at the plate. The coach throws pitches to the catcher. Some pitches will be strikes and others will be in the dirt. The runners practice game conditions and try to take the next base, while the catcher gets excellent practice at blocking the plate and throwing the ball quickly. The base the catcher picks to throw to doesn't matter; the idea is to have the catcher practice blocking and releasing quickly. Coaches should remind their young catchers to keep their mask on during this drill, as well as during games, while they try to throw runners out. Ripping off the mask is a waste of time. It is also unnecessary, since most modern equipment provides adequate sight of the ball. The catcher should be concentrating on getting the ball and throwing—and not putting an extra step into this process by worrying about ripping off his mask.

THE JOB OF THE BASE COACHES

As we stress how runners should trust their coaches and concentrate on their instruction, it is critical that coaches understand their own jobs. In general, coaches should not assume that players are aware of anything while they run. That means that coaches need to work while they have runners on base. Coaches' statements such as "They should know that" or "They should have been aware of that" are often excuses for coaches who are not working *their* position. Remember, good base running is a matter of runners digging in and following the signals of the coaches, rather than twisting their heads 360 degrees to assess and watch the play unfold as they run. Obviously, if runners do that, they may as well just sit down in the base path and wait to be tagged out.

THE FIRST-BASE COACH

The first-base coach has many jobs. This coach encourages the runner to run through the base. The instant the runner runs through first base, the coach needs to let him know if the ball was a hit or an out. Please, either way, communicate with your runner. In this communication, let the runner know which fielder has the ball. If the player is on first, then get his head in the game. As the play ends and the player rests on first, remind him of the following: (1) the number of outs, (2) that he should pick up the signals from the third-base coach, (3) the score, (4) the number of runners on base, and (5) to be thinking one base ahead—third base, in this case. Let the player know how important his hit or walk was. Finally, a good job for the first-base coach is to confirm the steal sign in case the player misses it from the third-base coach. After all, the third-base coach will also be flashing signs to the batter, so the runner may miss or be confused by the third-base coach's signs. Have your team rely on the first-base coach to confirm the steal sign by developing a simple secondary sign, such as having the first-base coach stand with his arms folded if the steal is on. If the first-base coach is not folding his arms, then the steal is off. This is a great safeguard system that allows your runners to double-check the sign.

THE THIRD-BASE COACH

The third-base coach is traditionally the transmitter for the offensive plays. This coach gives the hitting and running signs. He should also keep the signs simple. A system that works at all levels and one that doesn't get stolen by other teams is the "count" system. It's simple. Assign a number to each of your running and hitting plays (e.g., 1 is a steal, 2 is a hit-and-run, and so forth). Next, create an "indicator." The indicator can be anything, but it should be kept consistent throughout the season. The indicator may be a tip of the cap, or it may involve grabbing your belt buckle, rubbing your arm, etc.

The count system works like this: In this example, say play No. 1 is a steal, and your indicator is the action of grabbing the bill of your cap. You go through all kinds of motions, but you grab the bill of your cap only once. That gives the signal for play No. 1. If you grabbed the bill of your cap twice, then you would be indicating that you are calling for play No. 2, and so forth. The players should send an indicator back to the coach that they have understood the signal. The players' indicator can be obvious and simple because there is no need to worry about other teams stealing this sign.

In calling the signals for the game, there are some specific strategies that you can employ to your advantage. For example, if the grass is high, bunting may be more effective. If the pitcher is wild, then you may run a lot and, of course, take more pitches.

Similarly, if the pitcher throws a good curveball, then have the batters wait for the fastball. Always watch the opposing team's catcher during warm-ups. A good deal of your running strategy will be based on the strength or weakness of the opponent's catcher. Does the catcher throw well to the bases? Does the catcher fumble all over because he is encumbered by his equipment? Does the catcher fumble all over with his mask?

MORE PRACTICE DRILLS

Running and sliding are good for indoor practices. Have the players put on some long, heavy athletic knee socks while practicing indoors; the socks help make this practice fun and safer. Indoor practice is also conducive to demonstrating to the players the proper body position during both regular and head-first sliding.

When teaching the head-first slide, either indoors or on wet grass, coaches should teach the players to slide on their chest and keep their fingers relaxed and loose. Stiff fingers are prone to getting jammed against the base or against other players.

Chapter 7
Specific Strategies

JUGGLING THE LINEUP

Working with your lineup and your players maximizes your chances to generate runs and win games. A game plan that works well at younger ages is to put your best hitter up first. That player will get up to bat more times this way and will generate more offense in this position. This type of lineup lends itself to an aggressive running game and the manufacture of runs off a few hits. Let your best hitter get on with a hit or a walk, and then move them around with your running game.

Many coaches don't understand the interplay of a lineup. They just put their strongest player in the cleanup spot, their fastest player at leadoff, and their pitcher last. Setting a lineup is more complex than that. On an older team, a good leadoff hitter is a player with good speed who makes contact with the ball consistently and who is not afraid to take a walk. The second hitter has to be a good bat-control hitter. He should be able to take pitches, bunt, and ideally be able to go to the opposite field if he is a right-handed hitter or pull the ball if he is a left-handed hitter to move that runner from second to third. Speed doesn't matter as much for the second hitter in your lineup. The third hitter is the best pure hitter in your lineup. The cleanup hitter is your next-best hitter. The only difference between the Nos. 3 and 4 hitters is that the No. 4 hitter may hit the ball harder and get more doubles, triples, or home runs. The No. 5 hitter is much like the cleanup hitter, except he may not be as consistent as the latter. The No. 6 hitter is still one of your better hitters and resembles the No. 4 hitter. The No. 6 hitter might be a player who could be a leadoff hitter but doesn't run as well as the leadoff hitter. The No. 7 hitter resembles the No. 2 hitter. This batter can bunt and put the ball in play and can make something happen at the plate, but he may not be as fast as your other players. The No. 8 hitter is like the No. 7 hitter. This batter should be able to bunt, and should be particularly adept at the squeeze play. Ideally, this hitter has quickness and general smartness. The No. 9 batter may be a young player who you want to work into your lineup without putting a lot of pressure on him. This batter could resemble your No. 1 hitter—fast, puts the ball in play, not afraid to take a walk. The No. 9 hitter can serve as a second leadoff hitter.

In working with your lineup, play off your opponent if you have some familiarity with its players. If your opponent is going to start its best pitcher, then you may want to revert to your younger team or your running strategy. That is, you're looking to manufacture or "nickel and dime" this team for runs. You're not expecting to have big innings with big hits; rather, you're expecting to run and shake things up.

Conversely, if you are going to face a weak pitcher, get your weaker hitters into the game early and often to get them some confidence. You will be amazed at how these weaker hitters will come through for you later in the season if they build their confidence early on against weaker pitching.

ASSESSING THE OPPOSITION

We talked in Chapter 6 about watching the other team's catcher before the game in order to plan your running game. It is equally important to check the opposing pitcher as he takes his warm-up throws. Determine whether the pitcher is usually around the plate or wild with his deliveries. Your observations will help you to set your hitting and running game plan. Look at the opposing infielders as well, and see what type of arms they have. This helps you determine if you are going to take chances on the base paths. How are the arms in the outfield? Again, watching these players warm up will determine whom you will take a chance on. Watch how they field the ball. Do they juggle a bouncer out to the outfield grass? If so, you may want to take chances on keeping your runners going on a hit to the outfield. If you don't know the opposing team, you may want to wait until you can watch them warm up to determine your strategy, and therefore your lineup.

The third-base coach, the coach with the primary responsibility of calling the offensive plays, should be concerned only about scouting or assessing the opposition during warm-ups. Let your first-base coach run the warm-up, or have team leaders run the pregame warm-up. The third-base coach's time is better spent on getting a good, quick assessment of the opposition so that you can set your game strategy.

SETTING THE MENTAL ATTITUDE FOR YOUR TEAM AT GAME TIME

There is no such thing as a better team. That is the magic of baseball. In 1998, the New York Yankees set a record for wins in a season, yet every team in their division beat them at least once throughout the year. Did the

Yankees not try during those games? Of course they did. It just proves that any team can beat any other on a given day.

Coaches are the best models of how their teams are going to be mentally prepared to play the game. If you're positive and confident, that will rub off on your players. Young people look to adults and depend on adults for setting their attitudes. Coaching baseball is no different. Your players will watch you as you work with the umpires and the other adults at the game. So be careful. If you are disrespectful, unfair, or if you try to cheat, you can be sure that your players will adopt these same qualities in some form or another. They may not display these qualities today, but they will display them at some point, either during a game or during a practice. As their coach and role model, you will be the one who pays the price for their unsportsmanlike or negative attitude.

The most powerful and successful attitude you can foster in your players is one that shows respect for your opponents and the umpires, a desire to play hard and fair, and a penchant for following the rules of baseball.

(Coaching tip: Give each player a baseball rulebook. It not only sends a message to them about your attitude toward the game and how it will be played, but it also helps the players learn the rules of baseball.)

Baseball is a unique sport in that games can be won on a team's last offensive opportunity. The team does not have to beat the clock—only the opponent. As a consequence, baseball is a game of anticipation and reaction. A never-say-die attitude is a powerful message to send to your players, because it means that the game is not over until the final out. There is always a chance to win.

MOTIVATING YOUR PLAYERS

The motivation of the team starts with the coaches. If you are enthusiastic and positive, then your team will be. The best motivators are those that come from within your players, and the best way to motivate players from within is to lead them person-to-person. Communication with players and the use of affirmations are the best person-to-person approaches to use for motivating players.

When you talk to the team, make sure you begin from a base of respect. Put-downs, sarcastic remarks, bullying, or the drill-sergeant approach just doesn't work with today's youth. Oh, yes, for a very short time, a coach may get away with using this type of communication, but over the long

Specific Strategies

haul, it will fail him. These negative statements deflate young people's self-esteem and act as de-motivators.

Similarly, yelling is negative. If you have to yell at players, you will lose their respect instantly. But there is a difference between yelling and showing emotion and enthusiasm. There is nothing wrong with being enthusiastic and showing emotion. Yelling, on the other hand, combines emotion with negativity. Don't do it. Even though many of us were raised as athletes on this style of coaching, young people today are different and won't respond well to yelling. One of the most effective ways to motivate players is to respect individual differences. You will have a best hitter, you will have a best pitcher, and you will have a weakest fielder. Communicate honestly with all the players, both individually and as a team, on these differences. As long as each player on your team knows his role, he can rally around that role and be motivated to perform. But first, your communication as a coach has to begin with genuine respect and caring for the individual player. This challenge is just as great for the weak player as it is for the strong player. The weaker players need to know how much you are counting on them, and in what situations.

COMMUNICATING WITH PLAYERS

Along with this base of respect, the other most effective methods to employ when communicating with young people are honesty, genuineness, sharing, and mature, adult behavior. This last point is very important. Many adults who are thrown into the task of leading young people try to be a peer to these youth. But be realistic. Whether you are 25, 30, 40, or 50 years old, you will never be a peer of a group of teen or pre-teen players. When you try to be a peer, it presents a confusing and false image to your players. The players will respond to this image through a lack of respect and will undermine your leadership.

Also remember that the way you talk to your team will be the model for how they talk to you, to other players, the umpires, and the fans. If you swear, they will perceive that you allow swearing. If you disrespect the fans, they will also. Set an example that you are ready to live with in return.

This style of talking to players will make you more effective and powerful in your leadership of the team. Your players may need to be reprimanded from time to time, but if you follow our techniques here, you will find that your discipline will be more effective. Apply the communication principles outlined here and use the team consequence system as outlined in Chapter

3 when you need to reprimand your team. The more businesslike you are with the players, the more they will respect your reprimands. Young people will remember the consequence they had long after they have forgotten a coach who raged at them in a fit of anger.

MOTIVATION AND AFFIRMATIONS

Affirmations are a great way not only to talk to your players, but also to motivate them. What are affirmations? You actually see them and are affected by them all the time. The best example of the use of affirmations is the slogans that we hang in our locker rooms, schools, and gyms. For the Boston Celtics to put up their championship banners in the rafters of the Boston Gardens is an affirmation for the current team to succeed. For a high school football team to have a large banner hanging in the tunnel on the way out to the football field that reads: *"Winners pass through these doors!"* is an affirmation to succeed. Why do you think multimillion-dollar teams use these affirmations? Because they work.

Giving players a T-shirt with a positive slogan on it is an affirmation. Some adults think that these techniques are silly, but research has consistently shown that affirmations work extremely well in motivating people. The best evidence of the effectiveness of affirmations is their use over the years by corporations. Corporations use affirmations extensively, whether it is on company jackets or banners that adorn the plant. If big businesses are using this method, you can be confident that it works, because they are not going to throw away their money on something that doesn't provide a significant return.

Use affirmations with your team liberally. The team cheer is an affirmation, but so are practice uniforms, practice T-shirts, a team flag to put in the ground during practice and games, a team sign to put up on the batting cage during games, team wrist bands that match the color of your uniforms, or any other creative way to show the players that they are valued. In fact, your team uniform can be an affirmation. Making sure uniforms are worn properly, clean, and looking sharp makes players feel confident and effective. Use your imagination here and it will have big returns. Just ask large corporations.

One day during the practice for our 11-year-old team, a bus pulled up and baseball players filed out. As these players walked out of the bus, our players saw how resplendent they were in their uniforms, complete with turtlenecks with their names on them. Our players stopped practicing and

Specific Strategies

stood in awe. One player asked, "Who are they, a major league team?" In fact, this was an inner-city high school team arriving for a league game at that park. Some of these high school players were only a few years older than our 11-year-olds. The high school players looked motivated, confident, and ready to play.

Chapter 8

Coaching Pitchers

Coaching Pitchers

Coaches always seem to have a love-hate relationship with pitchers. This is probably because the personality of pitchers is unique to the position. Successful pitchers tend to be independent, intelligent leaders who can handle frustration and loss and live on the edge with risk. They are very much like quarterbacks of football teams. In fact, it is not uncommon to find that pitchers who also play football are also quarterbacks. These personality characteristics, coupled with the fact that the pitchers hold the game in their hands, results in their wanting to take things into their own hands. This is why they may sometimes be at odds with their coaches.

Coaches who are aware of their pitchers' unique traits will be better able to handle them during the course of a season. These personality types may allow you to pick out pitchers from the larger pool of players. Sure, you may have strong players who can throw the ball fast, but it is the leadership, intelligence, and frustration tolerance of the pitcher that will foster improvement. If a players just throws fast, that doesn't necessarily translate into his being the best pitcher on your staff. Many coaches and teams get burned by using players as pitchers who cannot handle the "heat" that goes with the job. These players pout, quit at the first sign of frustration, or otherwise act immaturely.

Your pitchers can be coached like your hitters. Weaker pitchers should be given opportunities to build confidence by getting them into games in innings where the other team's weaker batters may be coming up and you have a lead. In this way, you are not putting undo pressure on your weaker pitchers by putting them in a pressure situation. You always want to build confidence in pitchers, because it is a position of disappointment. Home runs follow strikeouts. Moments of success can turn to failure in an instant. For a player to be successful as a pitcher, it takes courage and confidence to be able to bounce back from these ups and downs.

Coaching Tip: Have pitchers watch videos of superstar pitchers that show how they can give up runs and still recover their composure. Watching players closer to their age can be more effective for some younger pitchers, so have younger players watch videos of college and high school pitchers having successes that follow failures. This is a good practice activity that can be done at home.

Coaching Pitchers

TEACHING PITCHING

There are some general guidelines you should follow when coaching your pitchers. For example, you should tell young pitchers that you want them to pitch strikes and let the other players on defense do their jobs. You also want them to get ahead of the batter in the count; pitching strikes puts them in that position. A pitcher should not throw the same pitch at the same speed twice in a row to a batter. Don't allow a pitcher to go on in an inning when the pitcher has already given up four or more runs. There is no character building by letting a pitcher get shelled. Take your best pitcher out when you have a six- or seven-run lead. Give your other pitchers a chance to get experience at that point. Use your bench vigorously.

PITCHING MECHANICS

To effectively teach pitching requires that you break down the pitcher's movements into small steps. The pitcher should start his windup with both feet on the rubber and his toes pointed toward home plate. The first movement that the pitcher makes is to rock back on the heels of his feet and move his feet to the right (for right-handed pitchers) or to the left (for left-handed pitchers).

Note: Teach right-handed pitchers to throw from the middle to the right side of the mound and left-handed pitchers to throw from the middle to the left side of the rubber. Because of the angle and release point, the ball will appear to be coming right at the batter's head. This angle can be a big distraction to the batter and also help the pitcher to throw inside to the batter.

The next action of the pitcher is to move his back leg and foot parallel to the rubber; in one motion, the front leg lifts and the knee is brought tightly straight up with a quick kick that almost touches the pitcher's chest with the front knee. The pitcher's weight is on the ball of his back foot at this point. This one-legged position is called the *balance position*.

While the legs and feet are performing these initial movements, the hands and arms are not idle. As the pitcher starts his rocking motion, his hands are being brought up to his chest. The glove and ball remain at his chest while he is in the balance position.

From the balance position, the back leg pushes off from the rubber and the bent leg begins to move downward and extend straight out down the curve of the mound. As the legs are pushing and extending, the hands begin to sweep downward, also with a push.

Pitcher at the Mound
(Right side for right-hander)

Ball Comes at Batter

The Balance Position

Hands Rise to Chest

Coaching Pitchers

These movements are now building the inertia of speed and power. The whole effort here is to gain energy to hurl the ball toward the plate with great force. So you see, performing the pitching movement correctly adds a great deal of power to the pitch. The more the pitcher departs from these movements, the more energy is lost.

Next, in a rapid movement, as the legs push off the rubber and the hand with the ball sweeps downward along the body, the pitcher allows the momentum of this downward sweep to push his arm and the baseball back upward and bring the arm into the over-the-top, 90-degree position. The forearm and ball continue this energized momentum and reach back away from the body in the classic pitching form. The gun is being cocked. The biceps and upper arm stay relatively even with the body, forming the 90-degree angle. It is when the forearm hits its farthest point backward that the momentum starts its movement toward home plate. As the arm and ball move toward the plate, the torso moves with it with a slight compact twist and downward lean. The chin acts as the targeting mechanism and points directly at the target (the strike zone) the entire time. Eyes also stay focused on the target.

As the ball and arm move past the body and down, the weight on the legs shifts from the back leg to the front leg, and the back leg kicks up. The weight of the body is now on the front leg. The ball is released when it is about belt high, and the arm follows through to a position that crisscrosses the body. The shoulder ends up even with the catcher's mitt. The body's momentum causes the pitcher to become off-balance at the front of the pitcher's mound, but the momentum of the back leg causes it to arrive quickly, almost parallel to the front leg; the pitcher is in a good defensive position, ready to field the ball. Ideally, this entire movement takes less than two seconds—1.3 seconds is great.

Coming off the Balance Position

Hands/Arms Sweep Down

Into the "Over-the-Top" Position

Ball/Forearm Cocked Back

Coaching Pitchers

Torso Movement as Ball Is Released

Head up—Chin Targets

Weight Shifts to Front Leg

Back Leg Drives Up

The Follow-Through

**Pitcher Finishes in a Defensive Stance,
Ready to Make a Play**

Coaching Pitchers

The whole idea here is to build speed and power through body momentum in the throw by using the body as the catalyst.

It is so important to teach this form to young pitchers. The pitching delivery should be top-heavy or over the top rather than side-to-side. A side-to-side delivery places too much stress on the elbow, arm, and shoulder. Young players may naturally want to throw sidearm, but you should try hard to cure them of this habit. Sidearm deliveries place a great strain on the arm, and they are also usually inaccurate. Players may have more speed with the sidearm at first, but at what future cost?

DRILLS

There are several good pitching drills that build proper pitching skills. These are the One-Knee Drill, the No-Stride Drill, and the Balance-and-Go Drill.

The One-Knee Drill consists of having the pitcher kneel on the ground with his knee opposite his throwing arm. Example: If right-handed, the pitcher kneels with his left knee on the ground. The pitcher throws from a distance about three-quarters of the way from home plate to the pitching mound. (Note: The distance will vary, depending on the age of the pitcher.) This drill teaches proper arm form, torso form, and follow-through.

The No-Stride Drill consists of having the player face the catcher with his feet about shoulder-width apart. The pitcher then throws (without using his legs) to the catcher. Teach the pitcher to keep his arm back and show the ball high in the air, rotating his torso while throwing to the catcher. Teach the pitcher to finish off the throw by crossing over his arm across his body and down. Again, you should do this drill from about three-quarters of the distance between home plate and the pitcher's mound. (Of course, the distance will vary according to the age of the players involved.) This drill reinforces proper upper-body movement.

The Balance-and-Go Drill puts the pitcher in the upright pitching position. The idea of this drill is to have the pitcher practice raising his leg in the windup position and holding it until the instruction from the coach to "go," or pitch. This drill helps to build balance and proper pitching form.

Finally, have your pitchers finish off this practice by throwing to a catcher in the squatting position and pretend that a batter is up at bat. This drill puts it all together: balance, stride, upper-body movement, and follow-through. Go through the balls and strikes for two to three pretend batters until the pitcher strikes each batter out.

Another important skill to teach in practice is the pickoff play. (This skill only applies to older players, when stealing and leadoffs are allowed.) Pickoff moves have to be practiced over and over so that they don't turn into balks.

DRILL

To practice the pickoff move, have your infielders rotate covering first base, second base, and third base. Have each one of your pitchers take a turn on the mound and have him throw a pickoff to each base. This gives your fielders good practice at taking the pickoff throw and applying the tag. You could even rotate your other players as runners on the bases so that they get practice getting back to the base, as we discussed in Chapter 6.

USING SIGNS WITH PITCHERS

For players who are younger, coaches will want to call each pitch the pitcher throws—without, of course, tipping off the batters. You can do this by developing a sign system with your catcher. Create a simple set of signs for each pitch your pitcher can throw. Use the same counting system we discussed in Chapter 5 and keep it simple. Train your catcher to give you a look after each pitch. Or, if the ball was put into play, have the catcher look at you for the next signal. Do not signal the catcher or pitcher verbally.

The One-Knee Drill   **The No-Stride Drill**

Coaching Pitchers

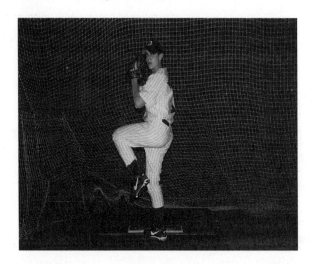

The Balance-and-Go Drill

You call the pitch, it is translated to the catcher, and then the catcher signals the pitcher. The advantage of this system is that it keeps the concentration of the pitcher in the game and on the target. It also keeps pitchers in a rhythm. The more your pitchers keep a rhythm, the more speed and accuracy they will put on the ball. This is good pitching mechanics. The windup is such a rhythm of momentum with the body that it makes sense to capture this same rhythm with the body between pitches. Try not to interrupt the pitcher's rhythm; instead, support it with your coaching.

Teach your pitchers never to express dissatisfaction at the catcher's calls, or the umpire's, for that matter. Open arguing with the catcher tips off the other team as to the pitcher's favorite or best pitches and gives the batters an edge.

Coaching Tips: At the beginning of the season, use your pitchers sparingly. Pitch them only about three innings (or about 28 pitches). This practice will save your pitchers' arms while, at the same time, giving them early-season experience. If you do use your pitchers for batting practice or an intrasquad practice game, start each hitter off with one strike. By doing so, you will keep your players focused and also help to move things along briskly.

Chapter 9

Now You Have a Team

Now You Have a Team

Coaching a youth team at any level involves strong leadership and modeling. Many people remember their coaches as very significant figures who entered their lives and fostered changes that lasted a lifetime. A coach might be one of the only adults a young person sees so close up interacting with other adults or with other youth. Players will scrutinize their coach's actions and reactions.

One of the most common relationships that players will scrutinize will be your relationship with the umpires. Realistically, arguing with umpires is an expected part of baseball. How you argue with an umpire can provide either a good model for your players or a negative model that they will take with them the rest of their lives.

Arguments as a good model? Heresy, you say. On the contrary, arguments and the way you conduct yourself in an argument are important and mature growing experiences for young people to observe. Where else can young people see adults have a disagreement and still cooperate to finish an event such as a ball game? Don't shy away from the need to disagree or argue with an umpire when it is justified. But be fair and respectful. It's OK to show your emotions, but don't denigrate the umpire as a person. That is a horrible model for the young people you lead. Conversely, if you argue fairly and powerfully, you will provide a wonderful model for the players to carry with them into adulthood.

For many reasons, instruct your players that you are the only person on the team who should approach the umpires. It is inappropriate for your players to argue with the umpires. Further, it is costly for anyone but you to approach the umpire. If a player argues, ejection from the game is automatic; whereas the unwritten rule is that a coach can approach the umpire and plead his perspective on a play. The same holds true for your other coaches. Umpires develop an instant negative attitude when your other coaches approach them. Why jeopardize a game by prejudicing the umpire against your team?

One of the times you will want to confront umpires is when they are inconsistent with calling the balls and strikes. A coach can call attention to such inconsistency by arguing the case with an umpire. This is a case where the squeaky wheel does get the oil. If you don't say anything, then surely, the inconsistent umpire won't change. However, if you keep calling the umpire on his mistake, at least you have him thinking about it.

Another time the head coach should argue is when the umpire makes a mistake with the rules. This will happen, because umpires are human, so always have a rulebook available to plead your case.

As a coach, you gain the most power in situations by being firm, in control, honest, and direct in your dealings with umpires, coaches, players, and parents. Keep this as a personal rule and you will be as effective as you possibly can in your communications.

One of the most difficult confrontations you will face as a coach will be the young umpire who will be calling your game. We advocate taking the high road with these young umpires. Do everything outlined above: be respect-ful, firm, have the rules ready. No doubt, you will see opposing coaches (unless they use this book also) try to intimidate these young umpires so that they get the calls they want. So what? If you are coaching to win at all costs, then you shouldn't be leading a group of young people. The essence of sportsmanship is to play hard and fair and not take advantage of some-one unduly. Intimidating a young umpire is a way of taking advantage of him—and it is unsportsmanlike. You should always consider the model you are presenting to the youngsters who are in your charge. By the way, we have seen intimidation of a young umpire backfire as many times as it has worked. Many of today's youngsters are spunky enough that they will passively-aggressively make you pay for your intimidation in some way.

Another of the common dilemmas you may face as a coach is coaching alone. This happens less frequently at the high school level and with teams associated with a school league. But sooner or later, at the little league level on down, you will find yourself as the only adult around at game time.

The beauty of coaching the way we have detailed it here in this book is that you will create a team that is intelligent and well trained. Because your team is so prepared as a result of the great practices you have held, being the only coach can provide you with the perfect opportunity to empower your players to step up and help you. Have a player lead warm-ups and pregame drills. Have another player coach first base. And following the guidelines we suggested in Chapter 2, you can designate a parent as the dugout coach. If you have employed the system of using parents that we offered in that chapter, you should have enough parents who are familiar with the team to take a role on a day when your assistants don't show up.

The synergy of our whole approach to running a team provides you with all the tools to cope with the unusual situations that may arise.

One note on coaching first base when your assistants can't make the game: Use a player instead of a parent substitute. Not only will a player be more in tune with the game because he has been practicing it with you, but the player will also know the other team members better than a parent will. Finally, using a player is a great morale builder for that player and the team. If promotion from within works in the business world, it certainly will work with young people as well.

IF IT AIN'T FUN, YOU'RE DONE

The bottom line for your team and for you is to have fun. The more you have fun with these young people, the more your enthusiasm will translate to them. Encourage your team to interact together and take the time to interact with them yourself. This will build team unity and make playing fun.

Young people's lives are vastly different from ours when we were young. Youngsters today are being shuffled from one activity to another. They typically don't have the time or ability to just hang around with each other, relax, and have fun. Creating this opportunity for your team will pay big dividends. You and your coaches will enjoy it also.

OFF-SEASON CONDITIONING

One of the ways to keep your team together, have fun, and yet prepare for the coming season is to encourage your players to meet for off-season conditioning.

A few words of caution are in order before your team undertakes an off-season conditioning program. For older players, your state high school athletic association may have specific rules about how you can encourage players to meet for off-season conditioning, *so please consult with your association before suggesting such a program.* For younger players, the physical work of conditioning may take a backseat to just meeting and having some fun as a team. This is not because we don't believe that younger players shouldn't be encouraged to condition their bodies; rather, it is because younger players should be allowed to be kids—to play other sports, to try other activities, and to have fun.

Now You Have a Team

Baseball is a game of speed and quickness. An off-season conditioning program should stress building these attributes. Plyometric training is an excellent way to build speed, quickness, and strength. Speed and strength training are very involved and require proper technique and supervision at all times. It is easy to become injured while doing some of these movements because they place the body in unusual positions.

In the off-season workout, include such plyometric exercises as the following:

- *Jumping rope.* This is a great speed, agility, and coordination builder.

- *Jumping the heavy rope.* Heavy ropes are available in sporting goods stores. They add strength training to the speed and agility building of conventional rope jumping.

- *Lunges.* Have the players walk across the workout area by extend ing one leg and bending at the knee until the lower body "lunges" forward in a way   that resembles a deep knee bend with one leg.

- *The box jump.* Place a small box on the floor and have each player stand to the side of the box. The player then side jumps over the box. Once the player lands on the other side of the box, he should bounce and side jump back to the starting side. Repeat over and over again.

- *The depth jump.* Take a short table or weight-lifting bench and have the players stand on the floor, facing the bench. Instruct the players to jump with both feet together up onto the bench or table and then back down to the floor.

- *Double-leg hole hops.* This exercise is like the box jump, except that it isn't done from side to side. Place a box in front of the players. Instruct the players to jump over the box with both legs, turn around, face the box again, and jump back over it.

- *Single-leg hole hops.* The movement in this exercise is the same as that in No. 6, except that the player uses only one leg at a time.

- *Ballistic push-ups.* Have the players do a push-up using two boxes or other objects under their hands to lift their arms and get a deeper push-up.

- *Cord or cable chest pulls.* This exercise is a conventional chest pull that builds upper-body strength.

Plyometric workouts are most effective when done by the well-conditioned athlete. Younger athletes should perform these movements carefully. Plyometric workouts should be limited to two workouts per week for no more than four intervals. It is imperative that the coach be diligent in his supervision of his players during these workouts.

Two of the most important body parts to strengthen for baseball are the abdominals and the lower back. So much of the movement of baseball starts with the abs and lower back. Make sure your players emphasize these areas in their off-season workouts.

On days that the players don't do the plyometric workout, encourage them to lift weights. An excellent weight-training routine includes bench presses, arm curls, lat pulls, back extensions, lateral raises (no higher than the shoulder), lateral pulls, squats, leg presses, quadriceps extensions, and hamstring curls. Strength training should be done three times per week and should be supervised. You should consult a trainer or one of the many fine books on strength training before implementing such a program for your team.

Chapter 10

Injuries and Injury Prevention

The most common injuries you will face as a coach are upset stomachs, bruises, scrapes, cuts, being hit by a ball, muscle soreness, pulled muscles, sprains, sore arms, headaches, and heat exhaustion.

In response to any of the above injuries, do not diminish the seriousness of the complaint. With any of these complaints, the worst coaching you can do is to instruct the player to "run it off." Although this may have been the common wisdom when you were coached, sports medicine has progressed to the point where we now know much more about effective alternatives.

Before we discuss responses to injuries any further, we need you to understand the importance of this topic. In today's society, with so many people entering into lawsuits, if you take a casual approach to a player's injuries, you can open yourself up to reprisals from parents. Therefore, you should always take the conservative approach to injuries.

For injuries such as sprains, muscle soreness, muscle pulls, swelling, sore arms, and severe bruising, the RICE method provides the best care. RICE stands for *rest, ice, compression, and elevation.* Get the player off the field immediately, have him rest, and follow the RICE recipe. The player may want to keep playing, but take him off the field, anyway. There is no benefit to having that player continue and, as a consequence, prolong the injury.

Many younger players will complain about stomachaches and headaches, and it is a fact of childhood development that younger children will have more of these complaints than older children. After all, younger children are still getting used to their body— particularly their body as it relates to sports. Again, don't push these players. You cannot possibly gain by pushing the complaining player.

The same advice applies to heat exhaustion. Heat exhaustion can have serious consequences and can even lead to collapse and death. Don't push players in the heat. Encourage them to drink plenty of water and apply cool washcloths to the neck and face. It's also a good idea to arrange for a tarp or other covering for your dugout area to provide some shade. Your team parents can help with all of this (see Chapter 2). In addition, you should substitute liberally in the hot weather and pay attention to your players' bodies. If they look lethargic, have them rest. If players turn pale or throw up, or if their body feels weak and rubbery and then they feel a chill and

Injuries and Injury Prevention

their eyes appear glazed and even roll back in their head, then get them to an emergency room immediately. These are the signs of heat exhaustion. Do not take them lightly.

Always stress eating well before a game. This is especially important in the hot weather, when young players don't feel like eating. Another time eating is very important is when you have a doubleheader. Instruct your players to pack a lunch for between games. Stress "pack a lunch," because you want them to take energy foods and not greasy fast foods or foods bought from unknown sources. The latter is a sure way to have a key player sick for the second game.

THE FIRST AID KIT

Bring a first aid kit to both practices and games. Items to be included in your team first aid kit include the following:

- Chemical ice packs

- Plenty of Band-Aids of all shapes and sizes

- Antiseptic

- Cool spray for players hit by the ball

- Splints for jammed fingers

- Athletic tape

- Ibuprofen and/or aspirin

- Ace Bandages of several shapes and sizes

- Pepto-Bismol or other stomach soother

- The numbers of the local emergency room and ambulance service

- Parents' phone numbers (keep a copy in the first aid kit)

- Visine or other eye drops to flush dirt or substances out of the eyes

- A portable phone for emergencies (packed in the kit)

Notice that we suggest you keep a copy of the parents' phone numbers in your first aid kit in the event that a player suffers a serious injury and needs medical attention. After contacting the emergency services, immediately call a parent. Further, if a player does suffer an injury that looks strange or serious to you, encourage the player not to move until you can assess the situation. For example, if a part of a player's body is twisted unusually after a collision or a fall, don't move the player. If a player complains that he can't feel or move a body part, don't move them. In both cases, call an ambulance. Always err on the side of caution. Even if the player ends up getting a free ride in the ambulance, at least you didn't risk permanent injury by moving a broken limb. You are not a physician; you are a baseball coach. So don't be a hero. Be overcautious on injuries that don't look quite right to you. Of course, if you happen to be a physician volunteering your time by coaching a youth baseball team, then this discussion may not pertain to you.

Chapter 11

It's Game Time

In the introduction, we emphasized that the thrust of this book would be on organizing and preparing your team and then holding great practices. Now that we are at the point where you have a team organized and prepared, let's discuss some techniques to keep you on the road to a successful experience.

TEAMWORK

The result of our efforts at team building and preparation should be a sense of teamwork that develops between you and your players. The point has been made throughout this book that your behavior as an adult role model will be copied by your players. Teamwork should be copied as well, and it will be if you set the proper tone.

Continuing your effective techniques of communication, motivation, and involvement will keep this teamwork humming throughout the season. A positive side effect of this team concept that results from teamwork is that it takes the pressure off the individual player. Many players quit baseball because too many coaches have individualized the game rather than stress the importance of the team concept. When coaching a team at any level, remember that the team didn't lose the game because your left fielder made an error in the last inning or because your pitcher threw the wrong pitch to their best hitter. You lost because your team didn't beat the other team throughout the entire game—not in just one moment in the game or because of one player. This team concept takes the pressure off individual players and allows each player to handle conflict more effectively. It also helps them deal with loss. The team concept gives the players a positive explanation for losing.

"There are 27 outs in a game. That we didn't get one key out is not why we lost."

Learning how to cope with frustration and loss is a great lesson for young players to learn about life. This type of lesson that young people can learn from baseball is one of the reasons why baseball has been such an important part of our society for so long.

PREPARATION

In this book, we have also stressed the importance of preparation in building and organizing your team. Now that you are ready to play real games, don't forget how beneficial this preparation has been. Develop and complete a *game plan* just as you did in preparing your *practice plan* (see Chapter 3). Assign the roles for the players on your team. Break down who is going to lead the team in warm-ups. Use every minute of pre-game time wisely. Write down the roles of your coaches so that you can spend your time analyzing the other team's strengths and weaknesses in an effort to formulate a smart game plan (see "Assessing the Opposition" in Chapter 7).

On the next page, we have mocked up a sample game plan. Just as an example, we set up this game plan as if it were for a school team.

GAME PLAN

DATE: 4-10-99__   OPPONENT: Billingsley

TEAM MEETING TIME: 2:45 p.m.__   GAME TIME: 4:30 p.m.

GAME LOCATION: Billingsley/ 92nd + Bridge Street

WEATHER CONDITIONS: Mild Temps-Fields still wet from rain yesterday

TIME:	PLAN:	NOTES:
2:45 p.m.	Meeting after school	Billingsley
	Last game with them.	
	#12 = 3/3 all to left-center	
	Same pitcher may be throwing	
	Look for all inside stuff	
	Possible lineup changes	
3:05 p.m.	Bus leaves for Billingsley	
3:30 p.m.	Arrive at Billingsley	Frank + Ken lead the warm-ups
	Coach Hayward—scout pitcher	
	Coach Mayer—scout catcher + fielders	
4:20 p.m.	Gather in front of our dugout	Last-minute instructions + Cheer
4:30 p.m.	Game time	

Notes:

Billingsley beat us last time with solid pitching and gap hits. Let's close those gaps today—adjust to the inside pitches. We were not awake last game—today let's be aware of their players' habits. After we win today and congratulate Billingsley, we will have a short meeting in our dugout, then board our bus. LET'S PLAY HARD AND HAVE FUN. IT SHOULD BE A GREAT DAY!!

GAME ATTITUDE

Game attitude is the same positive, motivating attitude that has been detailed throughout the pages of this book. Keep this attitude up throughout your games. Now, that sounds simple, but in the heat and competition of games, it will be very hard not to revert to the drill-sergeant approach. We hope we have made a strong case here that that type of coaching just doesn't work anymore—it doesn't work in practice and it doesn't work in games.

One technique that should help your team maintain a successful game attitude is to put the games in perspective for yourself and for your team. To do that, you may want to tell your players that the first few games of the season are the team's "spring training" games, just like those in the major leagues. These are the games where players are going to make mistakes and not everything is going to function like a well-oiled machine. By downplaying the importance of these early games, you can help to rid your players—and yourself—of opening-day and early-season jitters that inevitably result in errors.

Another good technique to keep the attitude positive is to use the first few games as your experimental time—a time to shuffle players into different positions and to lower your expectations. By doing so, you will transmit a more in-control attitude to the team, rather than create tension by jumping on your players' mistakes. Having your team's positions established from the first game on will bring with it a higher expectation. With that higher expectation comes pressure. Let the players fit into the team first. Even though we have made practices and organization more efficient, that does not mean that your practice decisions should be set in stone before the players take the field for the first game. For instance, you might observe in practice a player you think is fairly good at a particular position, and yet, he may not perform at the same level during a game. This miscalculation is certainly not an uncommon fact of baseball. Therefore, it is all the more important to use the first few games as a time to observe and experiment. Get your players into the early games and get to know the abilities of your reserve players. This relaxed attitude of yours should help you to build a successful team. The players will not feel as much pressure, and their confidence will build as they play and learn early in the season.

ONE OF OUR SUCCESS STORIES: SEAN LAWRENCE, OAKLAND ATHLETICS, 1999

We thought that a good way to conclude this book would be to demonstrate how effective our approach to building a team is by taking you through one of our many success stories.

Most stories chronicle the saga of the weak or mediocre player who builds himself up to the point where he becomes a success. But what happens to the gifted player who was always the player chosen first and was the star of every youth team he played on?

Sean Lawrence was such a player. When he was seven, Sean began to dream about playing in the major leagues. He had a natural talent for baseball, and, when he was a youngster, he always played on teams that were a level above his age group. Sean received a great deal of attention early on as a promising baseball player in a baseball program noted for producing good players and good teams. As a teenager, he was featured in TV interviews and received other publicity. Sean was on the fast track to a successful baseball career.

When Sean was 14, he played for Coach Steve Hayward (the coauthor of this book), and his Oak Park (IL) Pony League team finished third in the world. In the championship round, Sean struck out 17 of the 23 batters he faced. He also unselfishly accepted the role of closer for the team, even though he had always been the No. 1 starter throughout his youth-league career.

Then misfortune struck. Before his senior season of high school, Sean dislocated his shoulder sliding into a base. He did not play that season at all. Even so, Sean was rated the 10th-best player in the nation that year and received an athletic scholarship to Texas A&M University to play baseball.

Whether it was the result of his nursing his mending shoulder, or the effect of a year's layoff, Sean played very little at Texas A&M. As he put it, "Everyone all of a sudden seemed better than I was." Frustrated, he enrolled at the University of Illinois. To Sean's dismay, his experience at Illinois was exactly the same as his experience at Texas A&M. He did not play.

Upon this third setback and despite the great promise he showed as a youth, Sean wondered if his dream to play in the majors was now just a fantasy. Fortunately for Sean, his parents, who always supported him, had instilled in him the same never-say-die attitude that they carried in life.

It's Game Time

Instead of giving up, Sean realized that he didn't fit into the baseball program at Illinois and searched for a college program where he could play.

The father of Scott Spiezio, a friend of Sean's, drove Sean personally to meet with Gordie Gillespie, the head coach of the St. Francis College baseball team in Joliet, Illinois, and a legendary baseball coach in the Midwest. Sean enrolled at St. Francis and played for Coach Gillespie and played well.

After two productive years at St. Francis, Sean was drafted by the Pittsburgh Pirates in the sixth round of the 1990 draft. Now the story turns golden, right? Wrong. Sean's first year in the minor leagues was solid. But again, he suffered a major setback when he injured his knee and was unable to play for two years. Nonetheless, Sean was determined to achieve his dream. He rehabilitated his knee and returned to the Pirates' minor league system. However, even after finishing as the second-best pitcher in the league in AAA ball, he was not called up by the Pirates the following spring. Finally, after seven years in the minor leagues, Sean fulfilled his childhood dream when he was called up by the Pirates in 1998. He pitched three games as a starter. He won two of those games—two of only six victories the Pirates would chalk up in their last 22 games of the season. Even with that success at the major league level, Sean felt that the Pirates were not looking for him to fill a big role in the 1999 season, so he signed on as a free agent with the Oakland A's. Coincidentally, that move united him with Scott Spiezio, who also plays for the A's.

Sean Lawrence's story illustrates many of the lessons we have tried to emphasize throughout this book. In the end, he embodied all the characteristics of a successful baseball player: He overcame obstacles; trusted his coaches; tolerated his frustrations; displayed a solid work ethic; practiced hard; and was dedicated, motivated, and committed.

"Every general manager for every major league team is going to have to personally tell me I can't play at the major league level for me to give up my dream. Until then, I will keep working to pitch in the big leagues."

—Sean Lawrence, 1998

Safe!

The End!

Dr. John Mayer

Dr. John Mayer has been a practicing clinical psychologist since 1979. He received his degree from Northwestern University Medical School. He is a nationally known expert on the problems of youth and families. Dr. Mayer is a prolific author, lecturer, and consultant. He is the founder and director of both the Institute for Adolescent Development and the Center for Youth Research.

An athlete all of his life, Dr. Mayer has competed in over 20 triathlons and finished his first marathon. Using the techniques in this book, Dr. Mayer has been a successful youth baseball coach. Dr. Mayer is married and has a daughter, 18, and a son, 16.

Steve Hayward

Coach Steve Hayward has coached in the midwest for over 20 years. His manner and skills have become a legend among his colleagues and students alike. Coach Hayward has coached at the Little League, high school, and college levels. His Pony League teams went to the World Series four times. In 1987, Steve Hayward received the Amateur Baseball Coach of the Year Award presented by the United States Baseball Federation.

Coach Hayward is currently a scout in the Philadelphia Phillies Professional Baseball Organization, head hitting instructor at Strikes Baseball Academy in Broadview, Illinois, and he also represents the Stan-Mil Mitt Company throughout the midwest.

Coach Steve Hayward counts many current and former major league players as friends and colleagues. Many of his students are currently on the rosters of college baseball teams around the country. Steve is well known for his love of baseball. His rapid-fire wit and creative teaching techniques have developed young players who not only excel at the fundamentals of baseball, but also remain devoted to baseball and to Coach Steve.

Steve Hayward is no stranger to seeing his techniques in print. Not only has he been featured in many newspaper articles, but he also has written for such baseball publications as the *Coaches Digest*.

Steve Hayward is a resident of Oak Park, Illinois. He is truly a man who lives and breathes baseball.